POTTERY

Tony Potter

Edited by Jenny Tyler

Designed by Tony Potter

Illustrated by Chris Lyon and Guy Smith

Additional illustrations by Jeremy Banks, Janos Marffy, Peter Bull, Roger Stewart, Kuo Kang Chen, Justin Heath, Andrew Pagram and Mike Saunders

Consultant: Terry Robson

With thanks to Jill Crowley and Anthony Bennett

Contents

About this book

This book is a beginner's guide to making things from clay. The study of this is called pottery, or "ceramics".

Many people think pottery involves expensive equipment, but this book shows how you can make lots of things by hand with simple tools.

Although you need a special oven, called a kiln, to bake clay and make it hard, it is often possible to use a kiln at an evening class or school (there are more ideas on page 33). Alternatively, you can buy special "self-hardening" clays.

There are only a few basic skills in pottery and you can learn these by making the things in this book. To be successful, you need to take your time. Pottery is also a bit unpredictable – you can never be quite sure how something will turn out. This adds to the interest, as well as being disappointing when things go wrong.

There is a glossary of unusual pottery words on page 47.

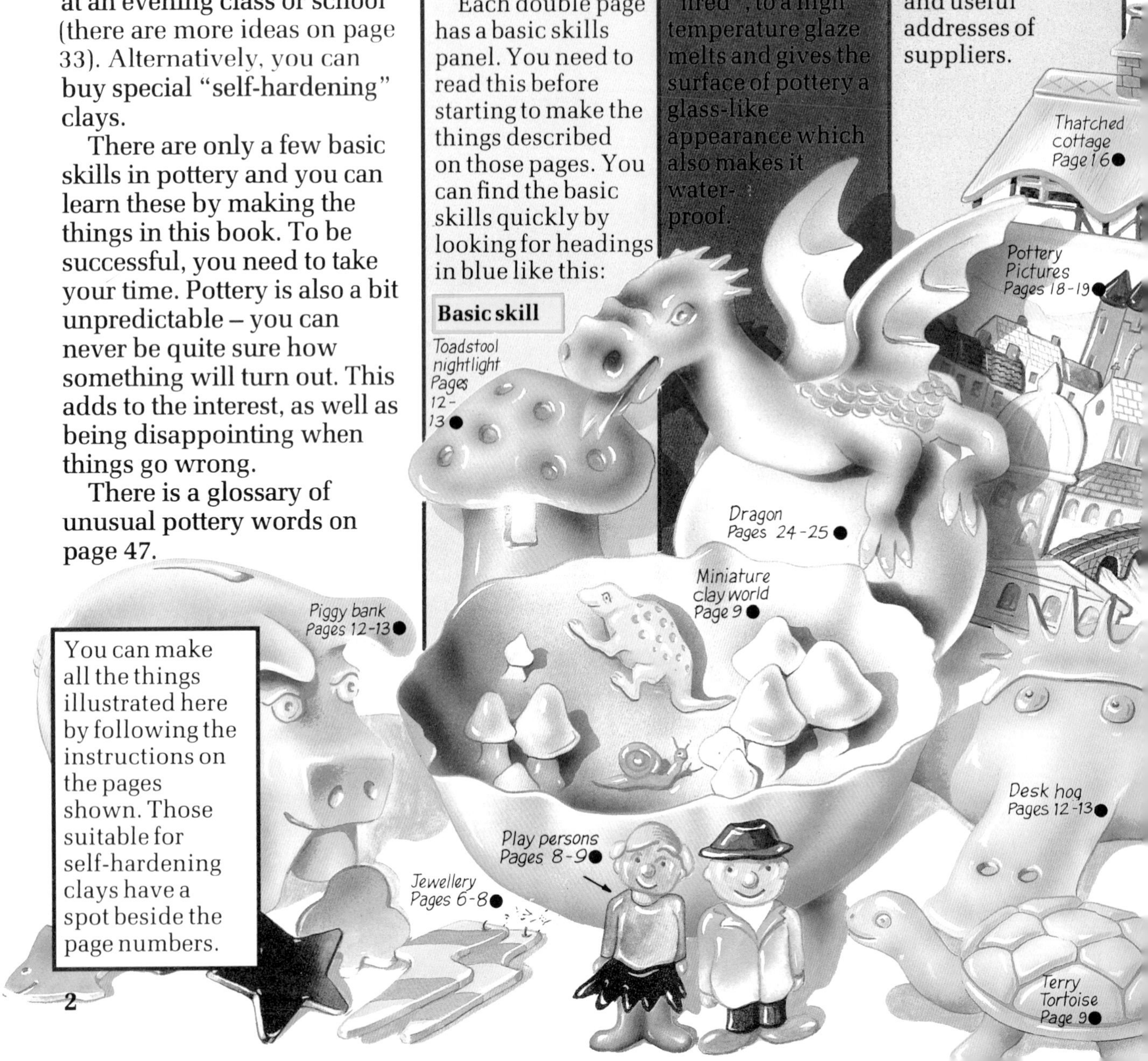

You can make all the things illustrated here by following the instructions on the pages shown. Those suitable for self-hardening clays have a spot beside the page numbers.

Using this book

This book takes you through all the things you need to know about making pottery, in three main sections. To find each one quickly, there is a coloured triangle in the top corner of the right-hand page, as described below.

The first section has yellow triangles and takes you through the basic skills needed to make all kinds of pottery. You will also find out how to make the things on these two pages.

Each double page has a basic skills panel. You need to read this before starting to make the things described on those pages. You can find the basic skills quickly by looking for headings in blue like this:

Basic skill

The second section in the book has red triangles. It shows how to decorate pottery with a kind of powdered glass called glaze, and other kinds of decorative materials too. When baked, or "fired", to a high temperature glaze melts and gives the surface of pottery a glass-like appearance which also makes it waterproof.

The last section has blue triangles. It has tips on designing pottery yourself and hints on how you might go about selling your work. There is also information on tools, materials and useful addresses of suppliers.

Thatched cottage
Page 16●

Pottery Pictures
Pages 18-19●

Toadstool nightlight
Pages 12-13●

Dragon
Pages 24-25●

Miniature clay world
Page 9●

Piggy bank
Pages 12-13●

Desk hog
Pages 12-13●

Play persons
Pages 8-9●

Jewellery
Pages 6-8●

Terry Tortoise
Page 9●

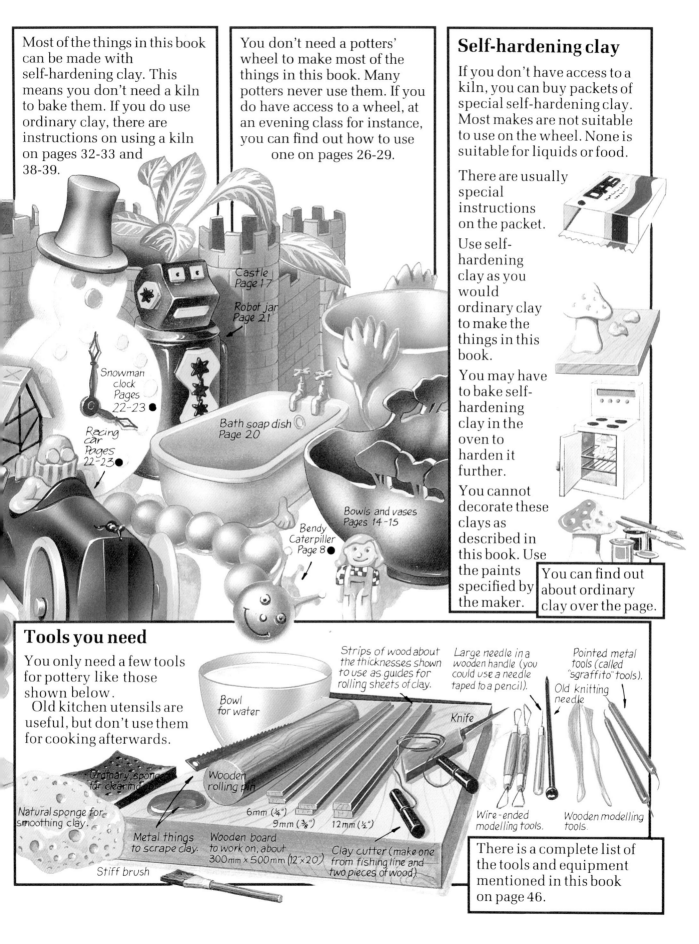

Most of the things in this book can be made with self-hardening clay. This means you don't need a kiln to bake them. If you do use ordinary clay, there are instructions on using a kiln on pages 32-33 and 38-39.

You don't need a potters' wheel to make most of the things in this book. Many potters never use them. If you do have access to a wheel, at an evening class for instance, you can find out how to use one on pages 26-29.

Self-hardening clay

If you don't have access to a kiln, you can buy packets of special self-hardening clay. Most makes are not suitable to use on the wheel. None is suitable for liquids or food.

There are usually special instructions on the packet.

Use self-hardening clay as you would ordinary clay to make the things in this book.

You may have to bake self-hardening clay in the oven to harden it further.

You cannot decorate these clays as described in this book. Use the paints specified by the maker.

You can find out about ordinary clay over the page.

Castle
Page 17

Robot jar
Page 21

Snowman clock
Pages 22-23 ●

Racing car
Pages 22-23 ●

Bath soap dish
Page 20

Bowls and vases
Pages 14-15

Bendy Caterpiller
Page 8 ●

Tools you need

You only need a few tools for pottery like those shown below.
  Old kitchen utensils are useful, but don't use them for cooking afterwards.

Bowl for water

Strips of wood about the thicknesses shown to use as guides for rolling sheets of clay.

Large needle in a wooden handle (you could use a needle taped to a pencil).

Pointed metal tools (called "sgraffito" tools).

Old knitting needle

Knife

Wooden rolling pin

Ordinary sponge for clearing up.

Natural sponge for smoothing clay.

Metal things to scrape clay.

6mm (¼")
9mm (⅜")
12mm (½")

Wooden board to work on, about 300mm x 500mm (12"x20")

Clay cutter (make one from fishing line and two pieces of wood)

Wire-ended modelling tools.

Wooden modelling tools.

Stiff brush

There is a complete list of the tools and equipment mentioned in this book on page 46.

How pottery is made

Making pottery involves several stages which are summarized on this page. Follow the numbers to see how you get from a lump of wet clay to a finished article. Look at this summary again if you want to check which stage to go on to next after making something.

1 Start by preparing the clay to remove any air bubbles. You can find out how and why you do this on the opposite page. All unfired clay in this book is shown bright red.

Clay

2 Next, make the thing you want. There are four basic methods to use, shown below, plus various combinations of them.

Piggy bank

See page 11

See page 17

Pinch pots – made by squeezing clay with your fingers.

Slab pots – made by joining flat sheets of clay.

See page 14

See pages 26-29

Coil pots – made with sausages of clay.

Pots made on the wheel ("thrown" pots)

3 Leave the clay to dry for about a day until it becomes "leather-hard", like firm cheese. There is a test over the page to help you judge when it is ready. At this stage you can finish fine details or decorate the clay (see pages 30-31).

Pottery objects are often called "pots" even when they are not containers.

4 After a week or so, when the clay is completely dry, you bake, or fire, the pot to about 980°C* to make it hard. This is called "biscuit firing". It also makes the clay porous for the next stage.

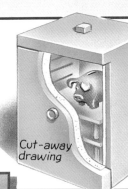

Cut-away drawing

5 The next stage is to cover the pot with a special kind of powdered glass called glaze. The powder is mixed with water, and applied to the pot by dipping, pouring, brushing or spraying.

6 Finally the pot is fired again; to a higher temperature this time (between 1000°C-1400°C depending on the clay). This is called glaze or "glost" firing. It makes the glaze melt and gives the pot an even, glass-like coating.

7 This is how the finished pot looks when it comes out of the kiln after cooling for about a day. The whole process, from start to finish, takes about two weeks.

About clay

There are two main types of clay, called "earthenware" and "stoneware". On this page you can find out more about clay and how to prepare it. You *must* do this before making anything.

Earthenware clay

Earthenware clay is porous unless glazed and fired to about 1140°C. It comes in a range of colours like those shown on the right. These are usually lighter when fired.

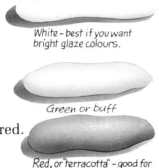

White – best if you want bright glaze colours.

Green or buff

Red, or "terracotta" – good for making unglazed flower pots.

Stoneware clay

Stoneware clay is usually non-porous when fired to its hardening temperature of between about 1200°C-1280°C. It comes in similar colours to earthenware.

White

Buff

Red

Buying clay

You can buy clay in 25kg (50lb) bags and smaller sizes too. It is best to buy the smallest size first so you can experiment and see if you like pottery. Start with earthenware, too, as this is cheaper.

You must buy glaze to suit the firing temperature of your clay (see page 34). Some kilns will not fire stoneware to its correct temperature – check the manual for the kiln you intend to use.

Preparing clay

Clay needs preparing before you use it to make sure its texture is even and that it is free from air bubbles. Air trapped in clay expands when heated in the kiln, causing it to explode.

The steps below show how to knead, or "wedge", clay to make it usable. It is always worth taking time to do this well, or you could spoil a whole kiln full of pottery.

Cut a piece of clay, the size of two large handfuls, with a cutting wire. Carefully re-seal the bag or the clay will dry out. **1**

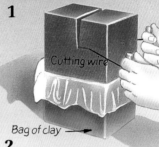

Cutting wire

Bag of clay

Pat the clay into a rectangular shape and position your hands as shown. Press down firmly with your palms, pushing the clay forwards. **2**

Put your hands on top.

Push this way

Prepare the clay on an absorbent surface

Roll the clay backwards (i.e. towards your body) and press down again – this makes a sort of "rams head" shape. Repeat this a few times. **3**

Press here

Lift the clay and start on the other side after a while.

Pat the clay into a ball, then cut it in half with a wire. Look closely at the surface to see if there are any air bubbles. **4**

Air bubbles look like spots.

Bang the two halves together as shown and knead the clay a few more times. Repeat steps 3-5 if you found any bubbles in step 4, until they are gone. **5**

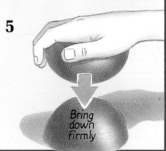

Bring down firmly

Jewellery, badges and key-rings

Here are some easy things to make by cutting shapes from flat sheets of clay. You could try the ideas on these pages, or think up some of your own.

You will need to buy extra parts, such as brooch-backs and earring wires, but these are quite cheap and can be bought from craft shops*. You will also need some strong glue, if you make a badge or brooch, to stick the metal brooch-back to the clay after firing.

First read the basic skill information below to find out how to roll sheets of clay to an even thickness.

Basic skill – rolling clay

Sheets of clay of an even thickness are called "slabs". Make them on an absorbent surface, like canvas or a wooden board, so the clay does not stick to it. This may leave a pattern on the clay, but you can smooth it out with a damp sponge.

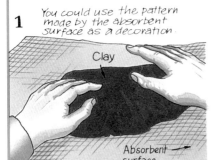

1 You could use the pattern made by the absorbent surface as a decoration.

Clay

Absorbent surface

Gradually flatten a lump of clay by patting it until it is roughly the thickness you want. You can also tap it with a rolling pin to do this.

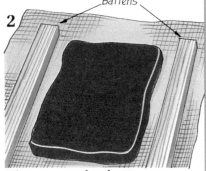

2 Battens

Place a wooden batten on each side of the clay. These determine the final thickness of the slab – the thicker the battens the thicker the slab.

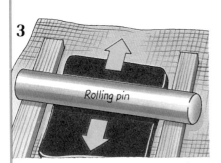

3 Rolling pin

Place a rolling pin on the clay and roll from the centre outwards. Then lift and turn the slab over. Roll and turn the slab until it is as thick as the battens.

4 Knife

Remove these patterns by smoothing with a damp sponge.

Leather-hard test.

It is usually best to let the slab dry leather-hard before using it. You can tell when it gets to this stage by cutting a piece with a knife to see if it is like cutting firm cheese.

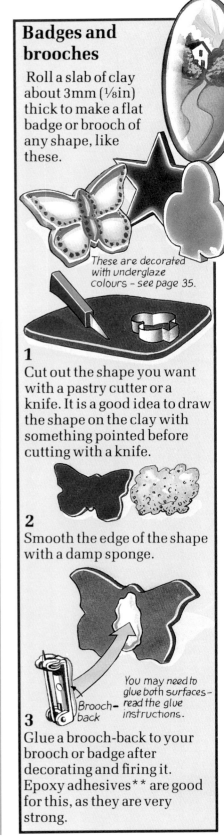

Badges and brooches

Roll a slab of clay about 3mm (⅛in) thick to make a flat badge or brooch of any shape, like these.

These are decorated with underglaze colours – see page 35.

1 Cut out the shape you want with a pastry cutter or a knife. It is a good idea to draw the shape on the clay with something pointed before cutting with a knife.

2 Smooth the edge of the shape with a damp sponge.

3 Brooch-back

You may need to glue both surfaces – read the glue instructions.

Glue a brooch-back to your brooch or badge after decorating and firing it. Epoxy adhesives** are good for this, as they are very strong.

*There are addresses of suppliers on page 47. These parts are called "findings".

**A two-part glue – adhesive and hardener.

Zig-zags

Use a slab of clay about 3mm (⅛in) thick to make these earrings. Follow the steps below twice to make a pair.

1

Make a tracing of one of the earrings above, cut it out and place it on the clay. Pierce through the outline with a pin to mark the clay.

2

Remove the tracing. Cut round the outline with a knife.

3 Make a hole in the top of the earring with a knitting needle or something similar.

4 If you like, scratch a pattern in the clay with a wooden or metal tool.

5 After firing, fix a jump ring* through the hole with pliers, then hook an ear wire (for pierced ears) or clip to it.

Key-ring

Follow these steps to make a flat key-ring of any design from a slab about 6mm (¼in) thick.

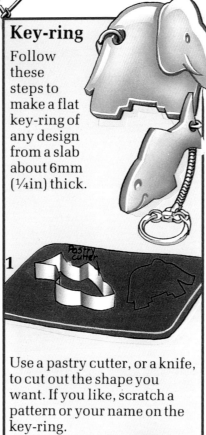

1

Use a pastry cutter, or a knife, to cut out the shape you want. If you like, scratch a pattern or your name on the key-ring.

2

Make a hole in the key-ring with a knitting needle or special hole-cutter. These are like apple-corers and are good for larger holes.

3

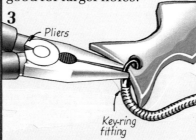

After decorating and firing, attach a key-ring fitting with pliers as shown.

Pendant

Make a pendant like this to hang on a leather thong or metal chain. Use a slab of clay about 3mm (⅛in) thick.

1
Make a tracing of the pendant above, cut it out and place it on the clay. Make the pattern by piercing through the tracing with a pin.

2

Cut out the pattern in the centre of the pendant first, using a knife. Then cut round the outline.

3

Decorate and fire the pendant. If you are using a leather thong, thread it through the hole at the top as shown.

*Jump rings are tiny wire rings.

7

Creepy caterpillar and company

You can make toys and ornaments by shaping and joining small pieces of clay. Look at the basic skill on the opposite page to see how to do this. To get you started here are some things to make – a "bendy" caterpillar, a tortoise and play persons to use in toy farms and so on.

You can probably think of ways of creating ideas of your own.

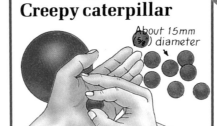

Creepy caterpillar

About 15mm (⅝) diameter

1 Creepy is made from small clay beads, threaded together with stiff wire. Start by rolling equal sized balls of clay in the palm of your hand.

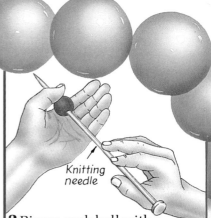

Knitting needle

2 Pierce each ball with a knitting needle (or something similar) when the clay is leather-hard. Then smooth them with a damp sponge.

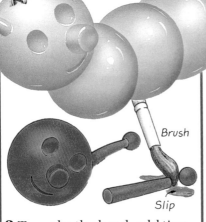

Brush

Slip

3 To make the head, add tiny balls and sausages of clay to one ball for the nose and antennas, joining them on with slip (liquid clay).

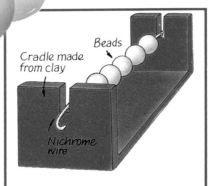

Beads

Cradle made from clay

Nichrome wire

4 Either glaze just the tops of the beads, so they don't stick to the kiln, or thread them on nichrome wire* as shown above, if glazed all over.

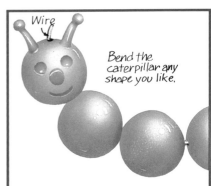

Wire

Bend the caterpillar any shape you like.

5 When glazed and fired, thread the beads together with stiff wire, bending the ends over with pliers to stop the beads coming apart.

Play persons

The pictures along the bottom of the page show some ideas for play persons. You can make them in any size up to about 50mm (2in) high. If you make them any larger, there is a danger they might explode in the kiln, as they are made from solid pieces of clay.

Sausages

1
Roll sausages of clay about 18mm (¾in) and 6mm (¼in) thick on an absorbent surface. See page 14 for tips on rolling clay.

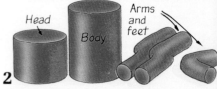

Head

Body

Arms and feet

2 Cut the sausages into pieces, as shown, for the head, body, arms and feet. (The feet are made from one sausage).

Wally waiter

Bill builder

Arthur railwayperson

Keith cook

Cyril clown

8

Terry tortoise

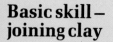

Terry tortoise is made from a hollowed-out lump of clay, with head and legs attached. You can make it any size (about 150mm/6in long looks good) and use it either as an indoor or garden ornament.

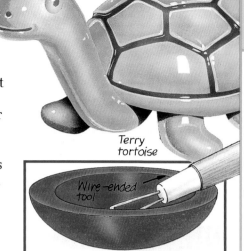
Terry tortoise

1 Roll a ball of clay in your hands the size you want, cut it in half, and scoop-out the clay from one half with a wire ended tool or spoon. Use the other half for the next steps.

Wire-ended tool

2 Roll sausages of clay for the legs, head and tail, large enough to be in the same proportion to the tortoise's body as shown in the picture above.

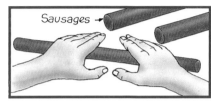
Sausages

3 Shape the legs, head and tail with your fingers. Then join them with slip to the inside of the body. Make sure the clay is well pressed together.

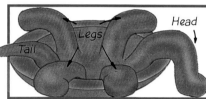
Tail Legs Head

4 Turn the tortoise over when it is leather-hard. Add tiny blobs of clay for eyes. Then carve the shell pattern with a pointed metal tool as shown.

Tool

Basic skill – joining clay

Unless very moist, pieces of clay will not stick together properly if just pressed. Clay mixed with water into a paste, called "slip", is used to stick them together rather like glue, as you can see below.

Clay Brush

1 You need a ball of clay of the same type as that you intend joining, some water and a stiff brush.

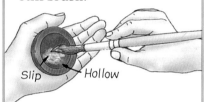
Slip Hollow

2 Press into the clay with your thumb to form a hollow. Dip the brush in the water and stir it round in the hollow. Continue adding water until you make slip about the consistency of cream. Make enough to use straight away, then mix more.

Surfaces

3 Brush the slip on the surfaces to be joined. Some potters prefer to scratch the surfaces first.

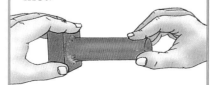

4 Slide the two surfaces together. Do this until you feel the clay begin to stick.

3
Shape the pieces with your fingers. Join the feet to the body with slip. Make pieces for the eyes and nose and join them to the head.

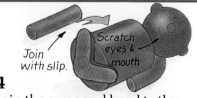
Join with slip. Scratch eyes & mouth

4
Join the arms and head to the body with slip. Then scratch any details, like hair, clothes and so on, with a pointed tool.

Tanya teacher

Brenda businessperson

Pam pilot

*This resists heat – see page 47. **9**

More earrings

You can make lots of fun earrings from sausages of clay. These work well if you stain the clay to colour it (see page 44), and then you don't need to use glaze. This saves time and money, as you only need to do one firing using this method. There are some ideas below which you might like to try. If you experiment you can probably design lots more yourself.

Candy stripes

You can make these earrings by painting them with underglaze colours or by using two stained clays, twisted together. Attach an ear wire (or clip) with a jump ring when fired.

1 Roll two thin, slightly tapering sausages. Then cut a length from each; one for each earring.

Knife

Cut the length you like.

2 Shape the thicker ends with your fingers to make them slightly fatter.

3 Make a hole in the fat ends with a needle, large enough for a jump ring (to fix ear wires to) to fit loosely.

Twist

4 If you paint the candy stripes, twist the earring while running the brush up its length.

Brush

Curlies

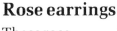

You can make flat, coiled earrings like these – any size you like. You could also make coiled brooches too by sticking brooch-backs to them.

1 Roll a long thin sausage. The clay should be quite damp to do this, or it will crack.

Sausage

2 Brush slip along one edge of the sausage.

Slip

3 Before the slip dries, roll the sausage into a tight coil. Cut off any excess clay to make it the size you want.

Cut here

Smooth hard

4 Smooth the end with a damp sponge.

Sponge

Ear wire

5 Make a hole in the edge for a jump ring, so you can attach an ear wire, or clip, to it after firing the clay.

Bolt ring

Cut-away picture

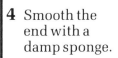

Rose earrings

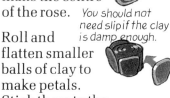

These rose-shaped earrings are glued* to studs (for pierced ears) or flat clips. You can also use them as brooches if you like. Make the roses any size you like.

1 Roll a tiny ball. If it cracks, start again with a fresh piece. Flatten the ball in your palm, with one finger, sliding it to make a rectangular shape.

The bigger the ball, the bigger the rose.

Push this way.

2 Curl the rectangle to make the centre of the rose. *You should not need slip if the clay is damp enough.*

3 Roll and flatten smaller balls of clay to make petals. Stick them to the centre, overlapping them as you go.

4 When the rose looks right, flatten its base with your finger.

5 After firing, glue the rose to an ear stud, like the one shown.

Ear stud

*Use an epoxy adhesive – see page 6.

Miniature clay worlds

You may have seen little pottery bowls in shops with 3-D scenes inside them. These are quite easy to make using a pinch pot (see the instructions on the right) for the bowl.

All the scenes are made separately and stuck with slip into the pot when it is firm, or almost leather-hard.

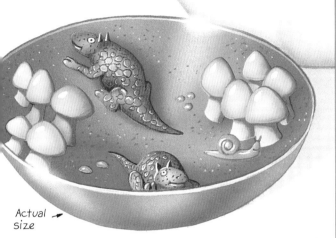

Actual size

1

Make a small pinch pot (about 100mm/4in across).

2 Shape these with your fingers

Make tiny creatures, buildings and so on. There are tips on page 25.

3 Brush slip here.

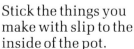

Stick the things you make with slip to the inside of the pot.

4 Details

Scratch any details in the clay with a tool when it is leather-hard.

Basic skill – pinch pots

Pinch pots are made, as the name suggests, by pinching clay with your fingers. The pictures below show the stages involved in making different shapes using this method.

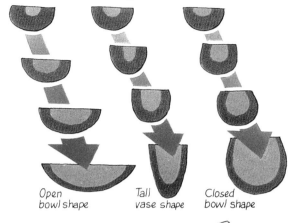

Cut-away drawings

Open bowl shape

Tall vase shape

Closed bowl shape

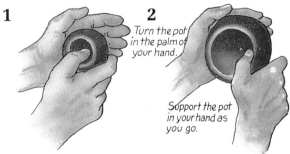

1

2 Turn the pot in the palm of your hand.

Support the pot in your hand as you go.

Roll a ball of clay in your hands, then press with your thumb to make a hole in the middle.

Squeeze the wall of the pot between your thumb and fingers, while turning it at the same time.

3

Always work from the bottom outwards.

4 Smooth with sponge afterwards.

Press edge of sausage with your finger

Continue squeezing the walls, in the direction you want them to go, gradually thinning them as you do.

You could add a base, called a "foot", by joining a sausage of clay with slip, as shown.

Piggy bank, desk hog and toadstool light

There are all kinds of practical things you can make from clay, like the ideas shown here. The same technique is used to make each of them – joining together hollow balls and cylinders of clay. You can find out how to make these by reading the basic skills information on both pages.

Basic skill – pebble pots

Pebble pots are two pinch pots joined to make a hollow ball, which can be altered in shape by rolling or tapping with a flat stick. Always make a hole in these, or the trapped air will expand and explode them in the kiln.

1 Roll a ball of clay. Cut it in two, making one piece slightly larger than the other. Then make a pinch pot (see previous page) from each piece.

2
Brush slip along the edges and press the two halves firmly together. Pull clay with your finger from the larger piece over the smaller one to join them together.

Piggy bank

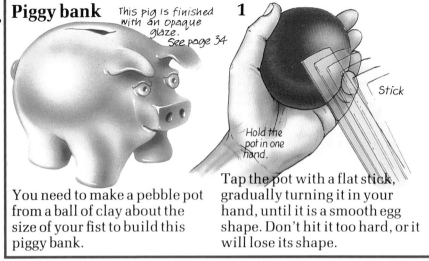

This pig is finished with an opaque glaze. See page 34

1

Hold the pot in one hand.

Stick

You need to make a pebble pot from a ball of clay about the size of your fist to build this piggy bank.

Tap the pot with a flat stick, gradually turning it in your hand, until it is a smooth egg shape. Don't hit it too hard, or it will lose its shape.

Desk hog

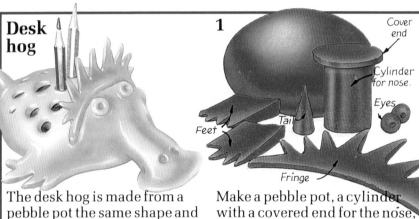

1

Cover end

Cylinder for nose.

Eyes

Tail

Feet

Fringe

The desk hog is made from a pebble pot the same shape and size as the piggy bank. You can use it to store pens, pencils and brushes.

Make a pebble pot, a cylinder with a covered end for the nose, and parts cut from slabs for the feet and fringe. Roll the eyes and tail.

Toadstool light

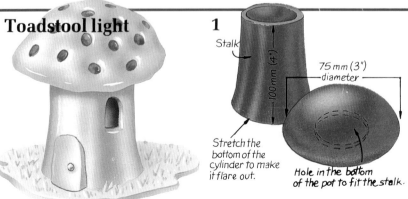

1

Stalk

100 mm (4")

75 mm (3") diameter

Stretch the bottom of the cylinder to make it flare out.

Hole in the bottom of the pot to fit the stalk.

The toadstool is made separately from the grass so that you can lift it off to place a small candle inside.

Make a pebble pot and cylinder. Flatten the bottom of the pebble pot by tapping it gently on a flat surface.

2

Make these bits as you need them.

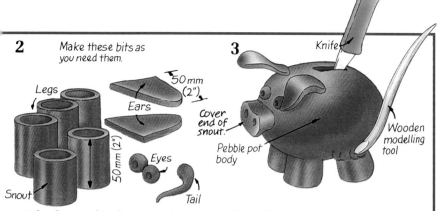

Legs

Ears

50 mm (2")

Cover end of snout.

Eyes

50 mm (2")

Snout

Tail

Make five cylinders (see basic skill on the right) for the legs and snout, cut two ears from a slab, and roll pieces of clay for the eyes and tail.

3

Knife

Pebble pot body

Wooden modelling tool

Join the legs and so on with slip, pressing a little extra clay along the joint with a modelling tool. Cut a coin slot in the back with a knife.

Basic skill – cylinders

You can make straight-sided cylinders quickly and easily by following the steps below. By adding a slab for a base they can be used as vases, or parts for other pots.

1

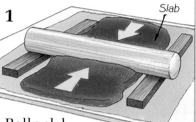

Slab

Roll a slab large enough for the cylinder you want to make.

2

Bottle

Tape a piece of paper as a "sleeve" round a straight sided object, like a bottle. Don't make it too tight.

Paper sleeve

Press along here.

3

Roll the slab round the sleeve. Cut it so the edges just overlap, brush slip along them, then press them together.

2

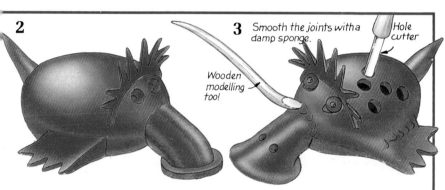

Join all the parts to the body with slip, bending the nose so that the covered end rests on the surface. You need to stretch the clay to do this.

3

Smooth the joints with a damp sponge.

Hole cutter

Wooden modelling tool!

Press a little extra clay along all the joins with a modelling tool. Make holes of various sizes in the body using a hole cutter or pointed stick.

4 Scrape the join with a flat tool to smooth it. Slide the bottle out of the cylinder when the clay is firm. Peel off any paper stuck to the inside and cut the cylinder to length.

2

Make a hole directly above the candle flame.

Hole cutter

Holes for light to shine through

Knife

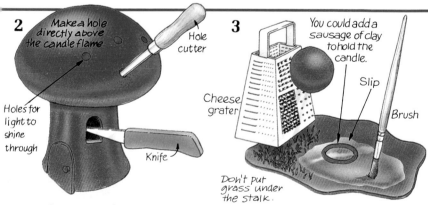

Join the top to the stalk with slip. Cut holes and windows for light to shine through. Add any details you like.

3

You could add a sausage of clay to hold the candle.

Slip

Cheese grater

Brush

Don't put grass under the stalk.

Cut the base from a slab of clay. Add "grass" by painting the base with slip, then shredding clay over it with a cheese grater.

Bowls and vases

Lots of interesting bowls and vases can be made using the method shown below. Those illustrated and explained on the opposite page are just ideas to get you started. These pots can take longer to make than those explained so far. There are some tips on page 45 on what to do if you cannot finish your pot in one go. Always make sure any earthenware pots you make to contain water are glazed on the inside, or they will leak.

Basic skill – coil pots

Coil pots are made from sausages of clay, called "coils". The coils are made into rings and piled on top of each other. The basic shapes that can be made by this method are shown in the pictures on the right. Follow the steps below to make coil pots of any shape.

Place coils directly on top to make a cylinder.

Overlap coils on the outside to make a bowl shape.

Overlap coils on the inside to make the wall cone shaped.

Combine the techniques on the left to make curves.

1 Roll a slab of clay about 12mm (½in) thick. Cut round something circular to make the pot base.

Glass Knife Slab

2

Coil

Roll coils of clay about 12mm (½in) in diameter. Roll gently, from the centre outwards.

3 Stick a coil to the base with slip, cutting it so its ends meet. Then press the coil to the base on the inside and outside as shown.

Coil Base Press the coils together.

4 Cut another coil and stick it with slip so its ends meet in a different place to the first coil. Then join the two coils with your finger.

Second coil Join here Press the coils with your fingertip.

5 Continue adding coils until the pot is the height you want. There are tips below showing how to keep it an even shape.

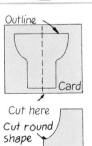
Join coils on the inside too Marks made by pressing coils

6 If the rim is uneven, trim it with a needle. Rotate the pot while holding the needle against it. Gradually push the needle in until the rim comes off.

Needle Something to rest on.

7 You can make a rim by adding a fatter coil to the top. Scrape the clay when leather-hard. Fill any imperfections with clay, then smooth with a sponge.

Scraper

8 Use a template (a kind of pattern) if you want pots to be even. Draw the outline of the pot on thick card. Cut the card in half.

Outline Card Cut here Cut round shape

9 Hold the template all round the pot after each coil to check and correct its shape.

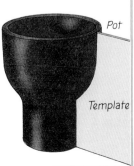
Pot Template

Flower vase

1 Coil a vase, the shape you like, as shown on the left.

Vase

2 Roll a slab about 10mm (³⁄₈in) thick and cut out petals, leaves and stems.

Petals

Slab

Stem

3 Stick the flower parts to the vase with slip. Use a modelling tool to squash the edges of each piece to the vase. When leather-hard, carve details into the flowers with a wire tool.

Carve details with modelling tools.

Crinkly-top vase

Make a tall cylinder with coils as shown on the left.

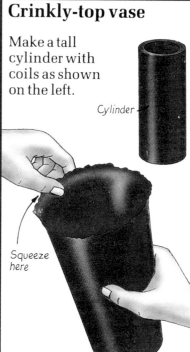

Cylinder

Squeeze here

Gradually turn the pot with one hand, while at the same time squeezing its rim between your thumb and forefinger to make a crinkly top. You may find this easier if your fingers are wet. Scrape the pot when leather-hard and fill any imperfections.

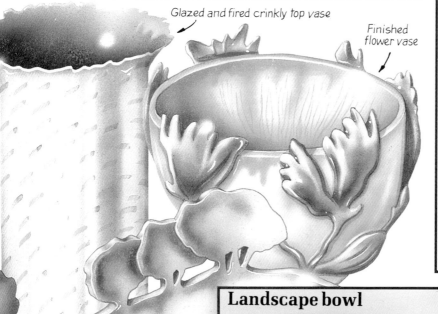

Glazed and fired crinkly top vase

Finished flower vase

Landscape bowl after glazing and firing.

Landscape bowl

1

Bowl

2

Knife

Line

Make a bowl the shape and size you want with coils. Allow the first few coils to firm a little before continuing. This will stop the bowl sagging.

Mark trees around the side, then cut along the line. Finish the trees by carving branches into the clay.

Thatched cottage and castle

The thatched cottage, which you could use as a night-light, and the castle plant pot shown here, are both made using the same basic skill. You need to read the basic skills information on the right before you start.

You could try designing your own pots too, based on the instructions given here.

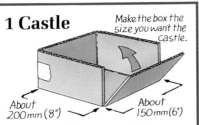

1 Castle

Make the box the size you want the castle.

About 200mm (8") About 150mm (6")

Cut up and re-assemble a cardboard box to use as a support for making the castle. This technique is very useful for making large slab pots.

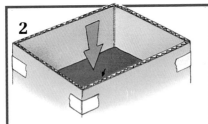

2

Cut a slab of clay for the castle base, the same size as the inside of the box. Then press the clay into the bottom of the box.

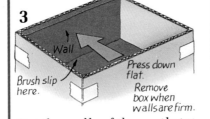

3

Wall

Brush slip here.

Press down flat.

Remove box when walls are firm.

Cut the walls of the castle to fit inside the box. Brush plenty of slip along the edge of the base and then stick them into position, one by one.

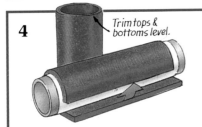

4

Trim tops & bottoms level.

Make four cylinders, big enough for the castle turrets, by wrapping slabs of clay over something round as shown on page 13.

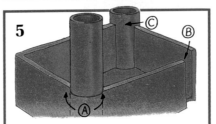

5

© B A

Position each turret and mark where they overlap the corners (A). Cut out the corners (B). Brush slip into each corner and stick the turrets in place (C).

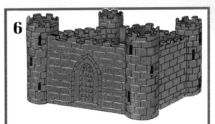

6

Use a knife to cut out the castellations, windows and so on. Carve the stones and other details using a wire-ended tool.

Thatched cottage

1 Cut five slabs of clay, about the size shown, to make the walls and base of the cottage. Join them together with slip, as shown on the right.

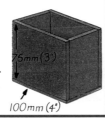

75mm (3")

100mm (4")

2 With a knife, first mark and then cut along the dotted line shown in the picture to make the shape for the roof.

Mark with a knife.

3 Cut a slab thinner than the walls and big enough for the roof. Drape it over the walls, shaping it with your fingers. Stick the roof with slip, unless you want a night-light.

Shape with fingers

4 Cut a strip from a thin slab. Brush slip along the top of the roof and fold the strip of clay over it to make the ridge. Slide it into position until it sticks.

5 Make a chimney by sticking together with slip the pieces of clay in the picture. Cut a gap in the ridge and stick the chimney in place with plenty of slip.

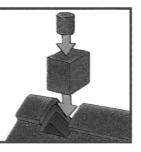

6 Mark and then cut out the windows with a knife. Finish off by filling any holes, carving the details and smoothing with a damp sponge.

For a night-light, leave the roof in place while firing.

Basic skill – slab pots

Slab pots are made by joining slabs of clay together with slip. This method is especially good for making things with flat sides, but you can also use it to make any of the shapes below. The steps show how to make a box, but the same method applies to other shapes.

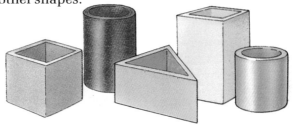

1 Roll out a slab of clay as shown on page 6. Let it dry almost leather-hard.

2 Cut out patterns from card for the sides and base of the shape you want to make.

Patterns

3 Place the patterns on the clay and cut round them with a knife.

Patterns

4 Brush slip along the two edges to be joined, then slide them together until they stick. Gradually join all the pieces to make a box shape.

Build on top of the base

5 Brush a little slip along each join. Roll out a thin sausage of clay and press it along the inside of the join to strengthen it.

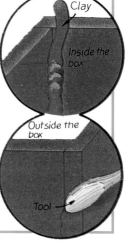

Clay

Inside the box

6 Smooth the joins along the outside with a wooden tool. You may need to use a little clay to fill in any gaps.

Let the finished article dry slowly – see page 45 for tips.

Outside the box

Tool

3-D picture and door plaque

By carving flat sheets of clay you can make 3-D pictures and door plaques. You could frame them, or fix them directly to a wall with tile cement or with a screw through a hole at the top.

Find out below how to carve clay, then follow the steps below and opposite to make the pictures illustrated. There are some alternative ideas at the bottom of the pages. You could make a whole sequence of pictures and hang them together in a line – perhaps telling a story.

Be careful not to screw pictures too tightly to a wall or door, as you can easily crack the glaze or clay.

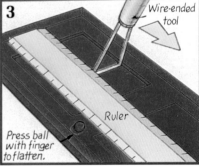

Basic skill – carving clay

Clay cuts neatly when left to go leather-hard. If you try to carve details before this, the cuts will make very rough edges. Here are some tools you can use to carve clay, though you can use almost anything.

1

Scraper

Bend here

Scrapers are flat pieces of metal, used to make surfaces smooth and flat. Hold them so they bend slightly in the middle.

2

Wire loop

Wire-ended modelling tools are used to gradually scrape the surface of the clay to remove a little at a time.

3

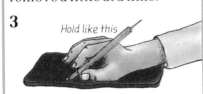

Hold like this

Sgraffito tools are held like a pen to cut fine details.

Door plaque

1

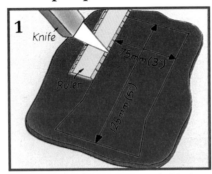

Knife

Ruler

75mm (3")

125mm (5")

Roll a slab about 10mm (⅜in) thick. Mark out a door and mat with a knife, using a ruler as a guide, about the size shown. Then cut round the shape.

2 Use the slab before it dries leather-hard.

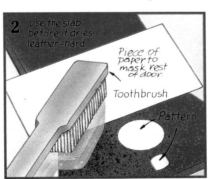

Piece of paper to mask rest of door.

Toothbrush

Pattern

Cut a paper pattern for any letters or symbols you want on the mat. Place it on the mat and tap round it with an old toothbrush to make a texture.

3

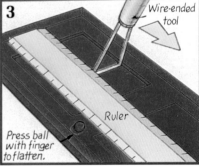

Wire-ended tool

Ruler

Press ball with finger to flatten.

Roll a ball of clay for a knob and stick it to the door with slip. When leather-hard, use a tool to carve the door panels, using a ruler as a guide.

This door-shaped plaque is finished with underglaze colours, followed by a transparent glaze – see page 35.

Alternative door plaque ideas

3-D picture

You make 3-D pictures by gradually building up slabs of clay in layers, as shown in the steps below. To paint the pictures, it is best to use underglaze colours, followed by a transparent glaze. The small details can be painted with a fine artist's brush.

Roll a slab of clay for the base about 6mm (¼in) thick. Cut out a rectangle about the size shown and use it before it dries leather-hard.

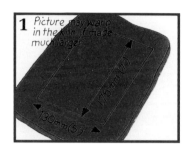

Roll a slab about 3mm (⅛in) thick and cut out the rough outline of the first layer of buildings. Brush slip on the back and stick it to the base.

Roll a slightly thicker slab of clay and cut out another layer of buildings. Position this, without any slip, so that it overlaps the first layer.

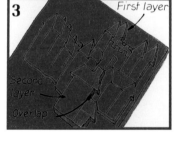

Mark round the second layer where it overlaps, then take it away. Cut through the first layer where marked and remove the clay to make a hole for the second.

Brush plenty of slip in the hole and press the second layer of clay into place. Continue steps 3 to 5 until you have made the complete picture.

Leave the picture to go leather-hard. Then use various modelling tools to carve details into the picture.

3-D picture strip

Bath soap dish and robot jar

Here you can find out how to make some unusual and useful things – a soap dish in the shape of a bath and a robot storage jar whose head is the lid. To help you make these things, first read the information in the basic skill section below.

Basic skill – using formers

A former is anything used to help shape slabs of clay. It could be a pebble or balloon, for example. You can also buy "moulds" to do this. These are made from plaster in particular shapes. Below are some points to remember when using formers.

1

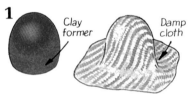

Clay former   Damp cloth

Slightly absorbent objects are best for formers because clay will not stick to them. You can use a non-absorbent former or make one from clay, but you should cover these with a damp cloth first.

2

Stretch clay over former.

Roll the clay out to the thickness you need and drape it over the former. Allow it to dry almost leather-hard before removing and using it.

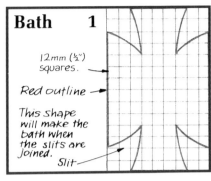

Bath   1

12mm (½") squares.

Red outline

This shape will make the bath when the slits are joined.

Slit

Draw a grid with 12mm (½in) squares, like the one above, on a piece of paper. Draw the outline shown in red. Cut round it to make a pattern for the bath.

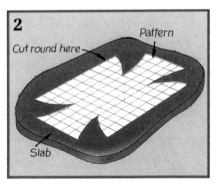

2

Cut round here   Pattern

Slab

Roll a slab of clay about 6mm (¼in) thick and place the pattern over it. Cut round the pattern with a knife. Remove the paper afterwards.

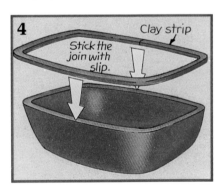

4

Clay strip

Stick the join with slip.

Take the bath off the former when the clay is firm and smooth the corners. Then cut a clay strip and stick it round the bath top to make a rim.

You could make a plug-hole for soapy water to drain away.

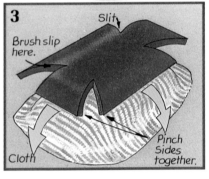

3

Slit

Brush slip here.

Cloth

Pinch sides together.

Shape a lump of clay and cover it with a cloth to use as a former. Drape the slab over it, brush slip in the slits and join the sides to form the bath.

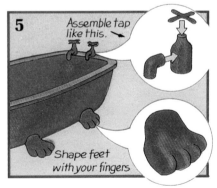

5

Assemble tap like this.

Shape feet with your fingers

Fill any imperfections with clay and smooth the bath with a sponge. Then make taps and feet from small pieces of clay. Join these to the bath with slip.

Robot jar

It is a good idea to decide what you want to store in this jar so you can work out what size to make it.

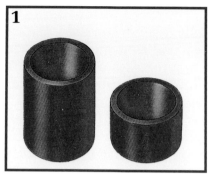

Make a cylinder as shown on page 13. When the clay is firm, cut the cylinder in two in the proportions of about a third to two-thirds.

Don't stick a disc on this end.

Trim round the disc after sticking it on.

Roll a slab of clay about 10mm (³⁄₈in) thick. Cut discs to cover three of the cylinder ends. Brush slip over them and stick the discs on.

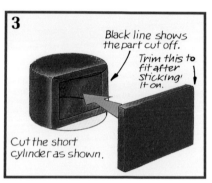

Black line shows the part cut off.

Trim this to fit after sticking it on.

Cut the short cylinder as shown.

Cut the smaller cylinder as shown. Then cut an oblong of clay and stick it with slip to the side of the cylinder. This part forms the robot's head.

Join here with slip

Strip of clay

Black line shows rim position.

Cut a narrow strip of clay. Cut this to fit inside the longer cylinder and stick it near the top with slip to make a rim for the lid to fit on to.

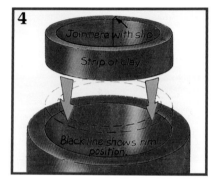

Things to use as formers.

Press clay with damp sponge.

Make or find things to use as formers for the lid bottom and robot's arms. Roll a thin slab of clay. Cut two pieces and drape them over the formers.

You must make a small hole in the head for air to escape in the kiln.

Trim the lid bottom and arms with a knife to give them smooth flat edges. Then stick them with slip to the robot's body and head as shown.

Smooth with a damp sponge.

Use pastry cutters to press out from a thin slab of clay any details you want, such as eyes, cogs, hands and so on. Stick these in place with slip.

Snowman clock and racing car

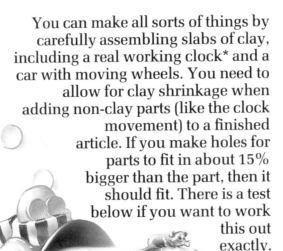

You can make all sorts of things by carefully assembling slabs of clay, including a real working clock* and a car with moving wheels. You need to allow for clay shrinkage when adding non-clay parts (like the clock movement) to a finished article. If you make holes for parts to fit in about 15% bigger than the part, then it should fit. There is a test below if you want to work this out exactly.

Racing car

1

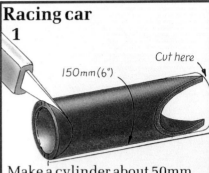

Cut here
150mm (6")

Make a cylinder about 50mm (2in) in diameter and cut the ends as shown.

2

Bend to fit.

Roll a slab of clay and cut pieces to fit over the front and sides of the cylinder. Stick them in position with slip.

Basic skill – shrinkage

Clay shrinks when drying and again during firing. This varies according to the type of clay, but is between 3%-12% in total. To work out the shrinkage rate, scratch a 100mm line on a slab of clay.

Measure the line after firing and do this sum to work out the shrinkage:

100 minus the length of line after firing = percentage shrinkage.

100mm
Wet clay

Bone dry

After glaze firing.

Metric measurements make the percentage easy to work out.

Snowman clock

2

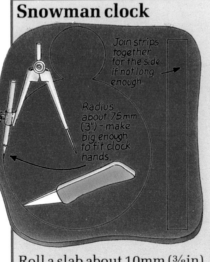

Join strips together for the side if not long enough

Radius about 75mm (3") - make big enough to fit clock hands.

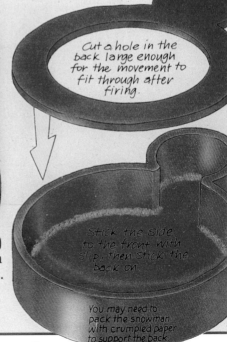

Cut a hole in the back large enough for the movement to fit through after firing.

Stick the side to the front with slip, then stick the back on.

You may need to pack the snowman with crumpled paper to support the back.

Roll a slab about 10mm (3⁄8in) thick. Mark out the front with a pair of compasses as shown. Repeat this for the back and mark out a side strip too. Cut the pieces out.

You will need to buy a quartz clock movement and hands from a craft shop (there are mail-order addresses on page 47).

3

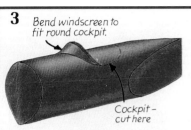

Bend windscreen to fit round cockpit.

Cockpit – cut here

Cut a hole for the cockpit (as shown by the black line). Then cut a small piece of clay for a windscreen and stick it in place with slip.

4

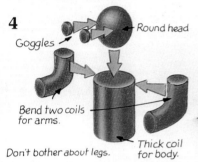

Round head

Goggles

Bend two coils for arms.

Don't bother about legs.

Thick coil for body.

Make a driver by shaping with your fingers the pieces shown and sticking them together with slip.

5

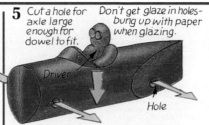

Cut a hole for axle large enough for dowel to fit.

Don't get glaze in holes- bung up with paper when glazing.

Driver

Hole

Turn the driver over when leather-hard and hollow out the inside. Then stick him into the cockpit with slip. Make holes in the car sides, big enough for 6mm (¼in) dowel (round wood) to fit loosely to use as axles.

6

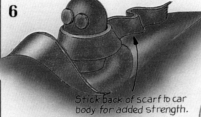

Stick back of scarf to car body for added strength.

Cut a thin strip of clay and drape it round the driver's face with slip to make a scarf.

7

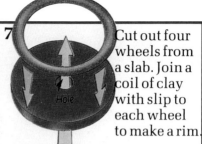

Hole

Cut out four wheels from a slab. Join a coil of clay with slip to each wheel to make a rim.

After glazing, cut two lengths of 6mm (¼in) dowel. Drill small holes through the ends. Assemble the car body and wheels with the dowel axles. Put washers between the wheels and body to stop them rubbing and use small nails to hold the wheels on.

8

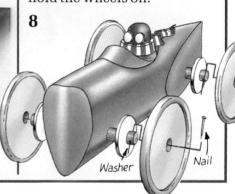

Washer

Nail

3

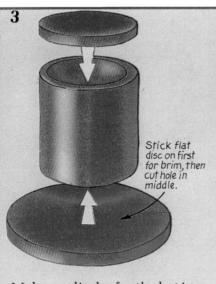

Stick flat disc on first for brim, then cut hole in middle.

Make a cylinder for the hat in proportion to the snowman (see page 13). Cut and stick with slip two discs of clay for the brim and top.

4

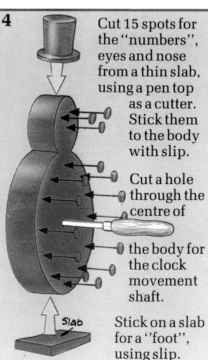

Slab

Cut 15 spots for the "numbers", eyes and nose from a thin slab, using a pen top as a cutter. Stick them to the body with slip.

Cut a hole through the centre of the body for the clock movement shaft.

Stick on a slab for a "foot", using slip.

5 Glaze the snowman with white glaze and paint the details with other colours*. Assemble the clock according to the makers instructions.

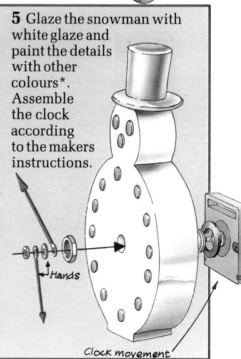

Hands

Clock movement

Dragon

You can make amazing sculptures, like the dragon below, by modelling with clay. Modelling involves shaping or carving lumps of clay with your hands or tools. There are some tips and suggestions on modelling in the basic skill section on the right. You might like to use them to work out ideas of your own.

How to make the dragon

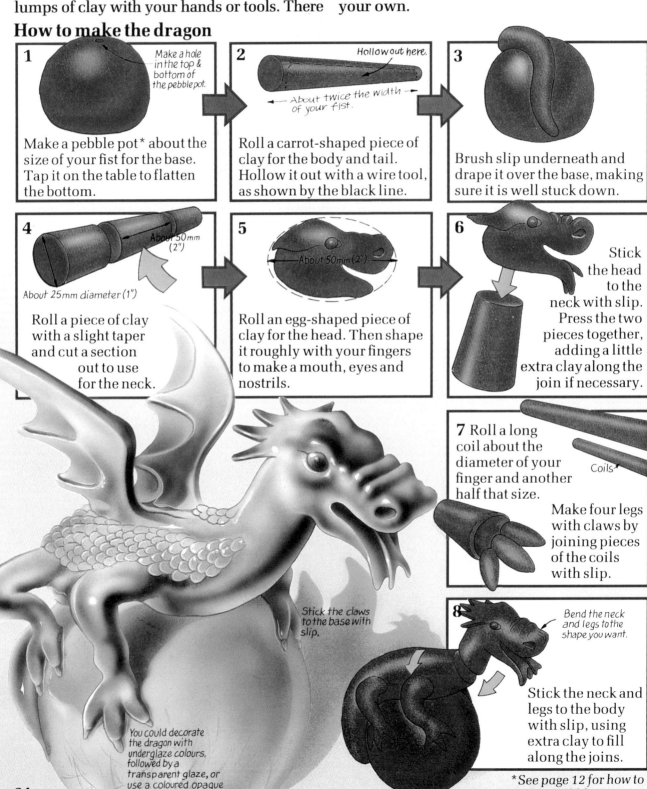

1

Make a hole in the top & bottom of the pebble pot.

Make a pebble pot* about the size of your fist for the base. Tap it on the table to flatten the bottom.

2

Hollow out here.

About twice the width of your fist.

Roll a carrot-shaped piece of clay for the body and tail. Hollow it out with a wire tool, as shown by the black line.

3

Brush slip underneath and drape it over the base, making sure it is well stuck down.

4

About 50mm (2")

About 25mm diameter (1")

Roll a piece of clay with a slight taper and cut a section out to use for the neck.

5

About 50mm (2")

Roll an egg-shaped piece of clay for the head. Then shape it roughly with your fingers to make a mouth, eyes and nostrils.

6

Stick the head to the neck with slip. Press the two pieces together, adding a little extra clay along the join if necessary.

7 Roll a long coil about the diameter of your finger and another half that size.

Coils

Make four legs with claws by joining pieces of the coils with slip.

Stick the claws to the base with slip.

You could decorate the dragon with underglaze colours, followed by a transparent glaze, or use a coloured opaque glaze – see pages 34-35.

8

Bend the neck and legs to the shape you want.

Stick the neck and legs to the body with slip, using extra clay to fill along the joins.

*See page 12 for how to make a pebble pot.

24

9

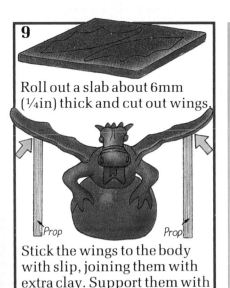

Roll out a slab about 6mm (¼in) thick and cut out wings. Stick the wings to the body with slip, joining them with extra clay. Support them with props if they sag.

10

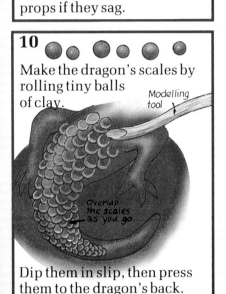

Make the dragon's scales by rolling tiny balls of clay.

Overlap the scales as you go.

Dip them in slip, then press them to the dragon's back. Start at the tail end.

11

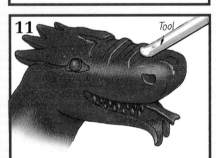

Tool

Add any details, like teeth and so on. When the clay is leather-hard, carve fine details with wire or wooden tools. Do this gradually, cutting away small pieces of clay to create the shape you want.

Basic skill – modelling clay

There are two basic ways of modelling, shown below. The first involves carving clay from a solid block to shape it; the second uses basic shapes as a framework (often called an "armature") to build on. You can also use a combination of these methods.

Carving

1

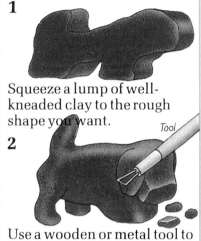

Squeeze a lump of well-kneaded clay to the rough shape you want.

Tool

2

Use a wooden or metal tool to carve the features of the object you want to make.

3

When the clay is leather-hard hollow out the object to leave a thin wall. Then use tools to carve any fine details.

Building

1

Pinch pot

Spacecraft

Slab

Slab

Pebble pot

Slab cylinder

Use any of the basic methods explained in this book (see page 4 for a summary) to form the parts of the object you want to make.

2

Join the parts with slip and add any extra details, shaped with your fingers.

3

Wire-ended tool

Finish the object, when leather-hard, by carving fine details with tools.

Here are some points you need to remember when modelling an object.

★Legs – Any object with legs or other thin supports is best made with a base of some kind to hold it up. The dragon's base supports its whole weight, not just the legs, for example.

★Always make sure there is a small hole in any part of an object where air is trapped, or it will explode in the kiln.

★Thickness of clay – it is always best to make objects with sides no thicker than about 12mm (½in). Hollow out the inside of solid shapes if they are thicker than this.

★Don't try carving fine details in the clay until it is leather-hard or you will not get a clean finish.

Using a wheel

Making pots on a potters' wheel is called "throwing". The name describes how the clay is thrown outwards by the force of the rotating wheel. By controlling this force you can make a huge range of shapes.

Throwing looks easy, but takes a lot of practice and patience to get right. On the next four pages you can find out how to throw a cylinder – the most basic thrown shape. You can also find out how to make handles which you can add to thrown or hand-built cylinders to make mugs and jugs.

If you would like to get really good at throwing, you can take lessons to develop your technique.

About wheels

There are two sorts of wheel: those driven by electric motors, and those powered by foot, called "kickwheels". Electric wheels are easier for beginners because you don't have to concentrate on what your foot is doing, as well as your hands.

To use a wheel, sit or stand at the front (some don't have seats) and rest your forearms, on the splash tray, where shown by the arrows below.

You need these tools for throwing. There are others too, but you can get by with these.

Rest your left forearm here

Natural sponge

Needle with wooden handle

Metal turning tool (see page 46)

Wire-ended tool

Bowl of water

Cutting wire

Wheelhead

Rest your right forearm here

Splash tray

On/Off button

This is an electric wheel. You can vary its speed with the foot control. Some have several fixed speeds, while others can be controlled gradually. A wheel like this costs about the same as a large colour TV.

Foot control. By pressing this you alter the speed.

First stages of throwing

The steps on the opposite page show what to do first, whatever shape pot you throw. This involves two stages: "centring" the clay to make sure it spins in the middle of the wheel without wobbling, and "opening out", to shape the inside base of the pot. You cannot throw a pot unless the clay is centred.

There is an indicator symbol like this to show the wheel speed at each step.

Slow   Fast

Preparing the clay

You must use well kneaded clay, of an even consistency, for throwing. It is impossible to throw properly if there are any air bubbles in the clay. To practise with, make six balls of clay, each about twice the size of your fist. Wrap them in plastic until you are ready to use them.

Hints and tips

Wear an old shirt or overall for throwing as it is messy. You may find it easier to take off any rings you wear, as they make ridges in the clay.

Avoid making the clay soggy by using too much water – you need just enough to stop your hands sticking to the clay.

Try to get your hands in the same positions as the steps show. You need to use lots of force for the first six steps.

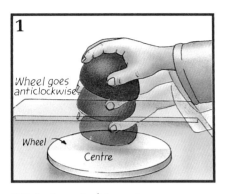

1 Wheel goes anticlockwise. Wheel. Centre.

With the wheel stationary, squash a ball of clay onto the centre of the wheel. If you miss the centre, slide the clay across and press it down firmly.

2 Lock your thumbs together. Only wet your hands if you feel the clay drag against them.

Wet your hands and the clay. Put your fingers around the clay as shown, then set the wheel going at high speed. Squeeze hard on the clay.

3 Rest your forearms on the splash tray.

Continue by applying hard and steady inward pressure with both hands. The idea is to form a flat-topped dome of clay which does not wobble.

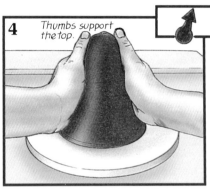

4 Thumbs support the top.

Change your hand position. Squeeze the clay and move your hands upwards at the same time to make a cone shape. This is called "coning".

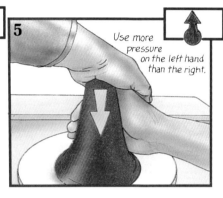

5 Use more pressure on the left hand than the right.

Alter your hand position. Push downwards with the left hand, while holding the clay with the right. The idea is to flatten the clay again.

6 Squeeze inwards to correct any remaining wobble. Don't take your hands away suddenly, or you will make it wobble again.

Re-position your hands. Press with your left hand to make the top of the clay flat. Try to keep the side straight with your right hand.

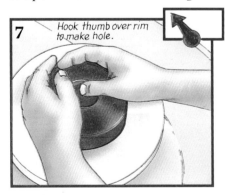

7 Hook thumb over rim to make hole.

Re-position your hands. Press with your thumb to make a hole in the centre of the clay. Support the side with the fingers of both hands.

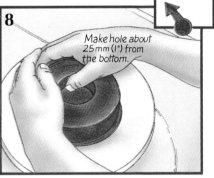

8 Make hole about 25mm (1") from the bottom.

Continue making the hole, lifting your right arm to get at the inside more easily. Don't make the hole too deep, or you will go right through.

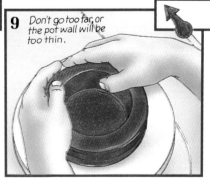

9 Don't go too far, or the pot wall will be too thin.

Pull the clay outwards with your thumb to make a wall. Support the outside with your fingers and left hand. This widens the inside of the pot.

Throwing a cylinder

This page shows how to throw a cylinder after reaching the last step on the previous page.

You can also find out on these pages how to remove the pot from the wheel. When the clay is leather-hard you can clean up the base to make it neat. This is called "turning" and is explained opposite.

There are also some tips on making jug lips and attaching handles to make mugs or jugs.

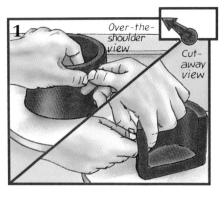

1 Over-the-shoulder view. Cut-away view

Bend the fingers of both hands. Squeeze between the knuckles of your right and left forefingers while lifting upwards at the same time.

2 Do this gently. Work from the right-hand side of the pot.

Continue lifting to make the pot wall rise. Keep your arms and fingers as steady as possible by resting your forearms on the splash tray.

3 This is called "collaring".

The clay tends to flare outwards. Position your hands to squeeze inwards, while lifting at the same time, to "pull in" the top of the pot.

4 You have to put your left hand right in the pot to start with.

Re-position your hands in the same way as step 1 and repeat steps 2 and 3 until the pot wall is about 8mm (3/8in) thick. Take your time.

5 Lift off the rim. Hold needle level. Support your hand.

Trim an uneven rim with a needle by pushing it through the rim. Lift off the rim when the needle goes right through.

6 Removing the pot
Press down with your thumbs. Remove any water in the pot with a sponge. Water

Clean the pot with a damp sponge. Splash water on the wheel, then draw a cutting wire under the pot. Do this a few times to release the clay.

7 The pot may lose its shape, but will regain it when you put it down. Put the pot on a wooden board, or "bat".

With dry hands, hold the pot around its base and lift it from the wheel. Place it on a board to dry leather-hard. Do this very carefully.

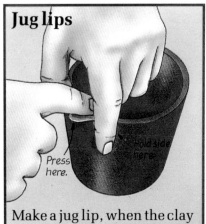

Jug lips
Press here. Hold side here.

Make a jug lip, when the clay is wet, by shaping it with your fingers as shown.

Turning

When the clay is leather-hard you can put it back on the wheel, upside down, to clean up the base and remove any uneven parts. This is done with metal turning tools.

You can either make the base completely flat, or cut away the clay to make a ring called a "foot". A pot with a foot is less likely to scratch any furniture you put it on.

Place the pot upside down in the centre of the wheel. Tap it until it is dead-centre. Stick it down with a sausage of clay pressed around the rim.

Sausage of clay

Do all the following steps with the wheel turning slowly. Hold a wire-ended tool as shown and gradually shave off the rough bottom edge to straighten it.

Tool

Start in the centre of the base. Hold a turning tool level and shave across the base with the point, moving it as if it were a record player needle.

Tool makes a spiral.

Carve a little way into the side of the base as shown in the two cut-away diagrams on the right. Don't cut too much – about 10mm (⅜in) wide and deep will do.

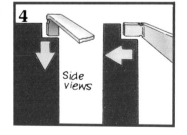

Side views

Hold the tool level again and gradually cut from the centre outwards to make the foot. Clean the pot with a damp sponge then remove it from the wheel.

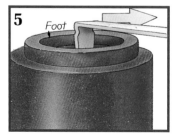

Foot

Making handles

Handles can be made by cutting strips of clay from a slab, but the best sort are "pulled", as shown below. These are much stronger than cut handles.

1 Squeeze a lump of well kneaded clay into a carrot shape. The larger the carrot, the bigger the handle. Hold it in your left hand as shown.

Hold in your right hand if you are left-handed.

2 Wet your other hand. Gently, but firmly, pull downwards, squeezing the clay between your thumb and fingers. Repeat this until the clay stretches to the size you want.

3 Cut the handle from the remaining lump by squeezing between your fingers and thumb. Place it on a board and leave it to go firm.

4 Brush slip on the pot where you want the top of the handle. Trim the thicker end of the handle with a knife and press it to the top of the pot.

Join with your thumb.

5 Brush slip where you want the bottom of the handle. Curve the handle over and press the end to the slip. Trim the end off if it is longer than you want. Finish the joins with a damp sponge.

Decorating unfired clay

There are various methods of decorating leather-hard pottery before you let it dry completely and fire it. You can draw patterns on the clay (called "sgraffito"), burnish it to make it shiny or press patterns onto it, for example. You can find out how on these two pages. Don't be afraid to experiment with decorating ideas of your own though.

There is also a stamp you can make to identify your pottery.

Sgraffito

Sgraffito means scratching the clay with a pointed tool. You can use almost anything, but special tools are made. Sgraffito is often done after applying coloured slip (see opposite page), glaze (see pages 36-37), or other kinds of colour (see page 35). You can also burnish the surface first (see below) to make it shiny and then scratch it.

1
Sketch your design lightly on the surface of the clay with a pencil.

Sketch

2
Use any pointed tool to scratch the surface or through the colour. The kind of line you get depends on the tool and the dryness of the clay. It is a good idea to experiment on scraps of clay with various tools.

Tool

Texture

You can easily change the surface texture of leather-hard clay. Here are some ideas.

1
Tap the clay with a stiff brush to roughen the surface.

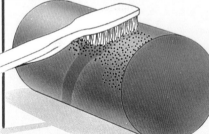

2
Paint thick streaks of slip to texture the surface.

3
Press a tool into the clay to make a pattern.

Wire-ended modelling tool.

4
Polish, or "burnish", the surface with the back of a spoon. You cannot glaze the pot if you do this.

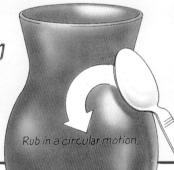
Rub in a circular motion.

Making a stamp

You can personalize the things you make by pressing a stamp into the leather-hard clay. You could make a stamp like this.

1 Sketch an idea based on your initials, or make up your own sign.

Sketch

2
Carve the design into a piece of leather-hard clay, or a scrap of wood. Biscuit fire the stamp if you make it from clay.

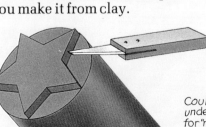

3
Press the stamp into the finished article.

Could stamp underneath for "maker's mark".

Could stamp here as a decoration.

Decorating with slip

Slip is liquid clay which can be used to decorate things, as well as stick parts together. There are various ways of using slip for decoration, some of which are shown below.

You usually need slip of a different colour to the clay used to make the pot. There are recipes below to make black, white, blue, green and red slip, but you can buy ready-prepared slips in lots of colours.

Slip-decorated pot

Slip-trailing

"Slip-trailing" is like icing a cake. You need a rubber bulb, called a slip-trailer, which you squeeze to suck slip into. You draw on the clay with it by gradually squeezing the slip out. It is a good idea to sketch your design with a pencil before you begin. Use a transparent glaze on anything you slip-trail.

Squeeze the slip-trailer, dip it in the slip and suck some up.

Slip trailer

Bowl of slip

Hold the slip-trailer upright, with the nozzle slightly above the clay surface. Squeeze it gently while tracing over your sketch. Remove any mistakes with a knife when the slip is leather-hard.

Pot on its side

Knife

Mistake

Spotting with slip

You can dip shaped tools in slip and press them onto clay to make a pattern – rather like potato printing.

Find tools with ends the shape you like, or make them from pieces of carrot cut with a knife.

Cut shapes with a penknife.

Carrot

Sketch your design with a pencil.

Dip the tool in slip and press it lightly on the clay.

Continue "spotting" with slip, using different colours if you like, until your design is complete.

Different colours

Dipping and pouring

You can cover all or part of a pot with coloured slip by dipping or pouring it over. It is usually best to use a transparent glaze afterwards if you do this.

To dip the pot, hold it upside down, as close to the bottom as possible. Dip it into a bowl of slip.

Container must be deep enough to cover pot.

Don't get your fingers on the wet slip.

To pour slip hold the pot over a container as shown below.

Pour slip from a jug.

Gradually turn the pot while pouring.

Slip recipes

To make slip for decoration, set up the things below.

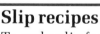
Washing up brush
Spoon

80s sieve (the number tells you how many strands of wire there are to the inch – the higher the number, the finer the sieve). See page 46.

Jug of water

Balance sieve on battens.

Washing-up bowl

Clay is the main ingredient. Leave it to go bone dry, then crush it into small pieces.

Mix the ingredients with water, put them in the sieve, then use the brush to press them through.

Allow the particles to settle, then pour out excess water. Mix the slip with a spoon to the consistency of double-cream.

Ingredients

White slip – 100% white clay

Black slip – 9 parts red clay 1 part manganese dioxide.*

Blue slip – 99 parts buff clay 1 part cobalt dioxide.*

Green slip – 98 parts buff clay 1 part chrome and 1 part copper oxide.*

Red slip – 100% red clay.

*See pages 35 and 46

Kilns and biscuit firing

"Biscuit" (or "bisque") firing means heating finished pottery in a kiln, prior to glazing it. This hardens the clay and makes it absorbent for the next stage when it is glazed.

Biscuit firing takes about 10 hours and reaches a temperature of about 1,000°C. The clay must be bone dry before you fire it. Various chemical changes take place in the clay during firing. Dry clay still contains water, which evaporates as the temperature inside the kiln reaches about 500°C. The clay shrinks a little as it is fired. Biscuit fired pots are often called "biscuit ware".

On these two pages you can find out about kilns and how to do a biscuit firing. After this you usually need to glaze the ware (see over the page), then fire it again to an even higher temperature (see pages 38-39).

About kilns

You can get kilns powered by electricity, gas, oil or solid fuel. Electric kilns are most popular and easiest to use. The kiln on the right is powered by electricity, but other types work in the same way.

Insulated case. This is lined with special bricks to prevent too much heat loss. Even so, the metal outer case gets too hot to touch.

Spyhole. You look through this to see inside when the kiln is on. It has a cover or small bung in it to prevent heat escaping. To see inside, move the cover with a stick or remove the bung with oven gloves. NEVER put your eye too close, or you will get burned.

Door catch. Make sure this is well secured when the kiln is on. Padlock the door shut if possible (some have special locks) to stop anyone opening the hot kiln.

Bung. A brick which fills a vent, removed during the early stages of firing to allow evaporating water to escape.

Heat-fuse. A safety device which cuts off the electricity if the kiln is accidentally left on too long.

Packing the kiln

Pack the kiln when you have enough to fill it. Remove all the kiln shelves except the bottom and the first set of props.

DANGER – Don't pack anything with air trapped inside. It will explode when heated.

Place pots close together. you can put small things inside larger ones, or stack things on top of each other, to pack the kiln as closely as possible.

Add more shelves and props to fill the kiln, leaving space for cones if necessary. Line cones up with the spyhole. Shut the door and remove the bung.

Pyrometer. A heat gauge which tells you the kiln temperature in degrees centigrade, usually on a dial or moving scale. You can use "cones" instead (see tips on the right).

Electric heating elements. These heat up in the same way as the bars of an electric fire.

Removable shelves and supports ("props"). These are made from special clay, called refactory clay. This can be heated to even higher temperatures than those used to fire pottery.

Temperature controller. This has various settings (like an ordinary oven) to increase the heat gradually.

Getting things fired

Kilns are expensive – the cheapest is about the same price as a colour TV. You can often get things fired quite cheaply at a pottery evening class or by a local professional potter*.

Checking the temperature

If the kiln has no pyrometer, you can find out when it reaches the temperature you want by using "cones". These bend when heated, as shown on the right.

You can buy cones to bend at different temperatures. A code is stamped on them (see below) to show their bending temperatures. The temperatures vary according to how fast the cones are heated. You need at least two, one for the temperature you actually want, the other at a grade lower to warn when the first is ready to bend.

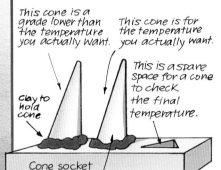

Cones are not re-usable.

Temp. is reached when the cone tip touches the surface.

Cone codes	Approximate rise of 60°C per hour.	Approximate rise of 150°C per hour.
08	945	955
07	973	984
06	991	999
05	1031	1046
04	1051	1060
03	1086	1101
02	1101	1120
01	1117	1137
1	1136	1154
2	1142	1162
3	1152	1168
4	1168	1186
5	1177	1196
6	1201	1222
7	1215	1240
8	1236	1263
9	1260	1280
10	1285	1305

This chart shows commonly used cones and their bending temperatures. Most manufacturers use the same code, but for slightly different temperatures. Ask for a chart when you buy them.

Using cones

This cone is a grade lower than the temperature you actually want.

This cone is for the temperature you actually want.

This is a spare space for a cone to check the final temperature.

Clay to hold cone

Cone socket

Place cones at an angle like this so they bend correctly.

Stick the cones in a "cone socket" with a small piece of clay. If you don't have a cone socket, just stick them in a slab of clay. Place them on a kiln shelf, directly in line with the spyhole.

Firing sequence

Most clays should be biscuit fired to 980°C. It is best to start firing early in the morning as it takes about 10 hours for the kiln to get this hot. Gradually turn up the setting on the temperature controller as shown on the right**.

Temperature controller

1 Check bung is removed. Switch on. 2 hours on low setting (0°C-200°C).

2 3 hours on medium setting (200°C-500°C).

3 Replace the bung. About 5 hours on high setting (500°C-980°C).

4 Check the temperature (or cones) regularly towards the end of the sequence. Switch off when the pyrometer or cones show the correct temperature. DON'T OPEN THE KILN.

5 Leave the kiln overnight to cool. Open the door a little at a time over a few hours to let it cool completely before removing anything.

*Look in the trade pages of your telephone directory to find a local potter.

There are various electronic devices available to control this sequence automatically. **33

About glazing

Glaze is a special kind of glass which sticks to the surface of clay when fired. You can buy or make (from raw materials) glazes in many different colours. Some are opaque and others transparent. Glazes can also be glossy, matt or semi-matt. All seal the clay to make it water-resistant.

There are three main ingredients in glaze: "silica", a glass-forming substance; "alumina", which gives body to the glaze; and "flux", which makes the ingredients melt and fuse together when heated.

The ingredients are in powder form. They are mixed with water and applied to biscuit fired ware. The biscuit ware rapidly absorbs the water, leaving powdered glaze on the surface.

On the next four pages you can find out how to mix and apply glaze and about other kinds of decoration used on biscuit ware.

Types of glaze

You need to use different glazes for earthenware and stoneware clays. Earthenware glazes are suitable for clays fired no higher than 1,150°C. Stoneware glazes are for those fired above this temperature.

Colours differ between the two main types of glaze. Stoneware glazes are usually very subtle, while earthenware glazes are much brighter. Colours also depend on firing temperature, the colour of the clay underneath and sometimes the position of ware in the kiln. Some glazes are quite unpredictable. The pictures below show samples to give an idea of earthenware and stoneware glaze colours.

Earthenware glazes

Examples of colours you can get →

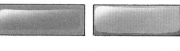

Stoneware glazes

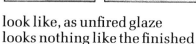

It is a good idea to glaze samples of clay so you can remember what your glazes look like, as unfired glaze looks nothing like the finished result.

DANGER

Always wear a face mask when mixing or spraying glaze and similar materials as the dust can be poisonous. Use a damp cloth to wipe dust from surfaces so as not to spread it.

Preparing glazes

80s sieve (The number tells you how many strands of wire there are to the inch – the higher the number, the finer the sieve).

Two containers

Two wooden battens

Stiff washing-up brush

Wooden spoon or stick

Follow the steps on the right to prepare ready-mixed powdered glaze. The picture above shows the things you need to do this.

Buying glaze

You can buy glaze in three ways, as shown below.

Ready-prepared, or "slop", glazes are the easiest to use as they are already mixed with water, but they are expensive.

You can prepare glaze from ready-mixed ingredients. These are cheaper than slop glazes. The steps at the bottom of these pages show how to prepare them.

Slop glazes

Ready mixed ingredients

Powdered ingredients

You can also buy the basic ingredients to make up your own glazes from recipes*. This is the most difficult method, but a good idea if you want to experiment.

Other kinds of decoration

You can use the materials described below to decorate under or over glaze. Most are made from "oxides" – a raw colouring pigment, with various other ingredients added. When you buy them it is best to ask for instructions, as they vary according to the manufacturer. They are usually mixed with water and painted on with a brush.

The pictures below show the kinds of colours you can get by using these materials on white clay with a transparent glaze on top. The darker the clay, the darker the colours will be. You need to experiment on the clay you use.

Oxides

With oxides you can paint designs onto unfired or biscuit fired ware, either before or after glazing. The pictures on the right show commonly used oxides.

Stains

Stains are prepared oxides, in a range of predictable colours. Those on the right are examples of the colours you can get.

Underglaze colours

These usually come in tubes, as felt pens, or as crayons. You use them to paint or draw on unfired or biscuit fired clay. Glaze on top of them with a transparent glaze.

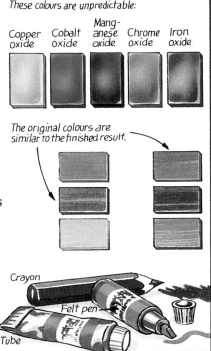

These colours are unpredictable:

Copper oxide · Cobalt oxide · Manganese oxide · Chrome oxide · Iron oxide

The original colours are similar to the finished result.

Crayon

Felt pen

Tube

---

1 Put the powder in a container. Add a little water and mix it with a spoon to make a paste.

Water

Spoon

Glaze

Must be well mixed.

Bucket

Add more water, stirring as you go, until the mixture is like single cream.

2 Pour the glaze into the sieve, gently brushing it through.

Brush

Sieve

3 Arrange the sieve over the empty container and pour the glaze through again.

Glaze

Store the glaze in a lidded container. Always stir it before use.

Some books with recipes are suggested on page 47.

How to glaze

There are four basic ways of applying glaze; by dipping, pouring, brushing and spraying. The steps on these pages show what to do. The method you choose affects the look of the finished article. Spraying gives a more even finish than the other techniques.

Glaze needs to be about 2mm (1/10in) thick. You may need more than one coat to make it thick enough. At this stage the glaze is very fragile – avoid touching it if possible.

Hints and tips

★Avoid handling ware too much or grease from your fingers will prevent the glaze from sticking.

★Wash dusty biscuit ware under the tap.

★Pots must be completely dry before glazing.

★Remove dribbles of glaze by gently rubbing them with your finger when the glaze is dry.

★Touch-up damaged areas of glaze with a blob of the same colour on a brush.

★To glaze over oxides and some stains and underglaze colours you may need to use a spraygun to prevent smudging. Some colours contain gum which help prevent this happening.

Cleaning the base

Always clean the base with a wet sponge after glazing, or the pot will stick to the kiln. Wipe off glaze around the base too, in case it drips.

Dipping

Put the glaze in a container wide and deep enough to dip your work in. Stir the glaze and make sure there are no thick bits at the bottom of the container.

Hold the pot near its base. If you can't do this, dip it half-way, then do the other half. If the pot is large enough, you may be able to put your hand inside to hold it.

Dip the pot right into the glaze, up to your fingers.

Hold it there for a couple of seconds, then take it out.

Glaze

Let drips fall into the container.

Glaze lightens in colour when dry.

When the glaze looks dry (after about 30 seconds), put the pot down on a flat surface.

Pouring

Pour glaze over your pot if its shape makes it difficult to dip. Glaze the insides of pots by pouring too.

Pour the glaze in a jug.

Glaze

Hold your pot over a bowl large enough to catch the drips. Then gradually pour glaze over the part you are not holding.

Shake the drips off.

When the glaze looks dry (after about 30 seconds), hold the glazed part and pour glaze over the blank area.

Glaze inside a pot by pouring it in from a jug. Swill the glaze around, up to the rim, then quickly pour it out into a bowl.

Painting

Applying glaze evenly with a brush is difficult, especially on large areas. You can buy special brush-on glazes, mixed with gum to make this easier. Painting works well on small areas.

It is a good idea to use a turntable called a "banding wheel" when painting glazes (and other decorations).

Use a soft brush, well loaded with glaze, for painting. There are special types you can buy called "mop" brushes.

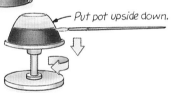

Put pot upside down.

To glaze an entire pot, start at the top, spinning the wheel as you go. You may need to use several coats of glaze.

If you want to paint lots of fine details it is a good idea to use underglaze colours (see page 35), followed by a transparent glaze.

Hold brush upright.

Try to keep the brush well loaded rather than dragging it across the surface.

Spraying

Glaze can be sprayed through any type of spraygun (see page 46). You also need a "spray booth" with an extractor fan to suck up particles in the air. Spraying equipment is expensive, but you could use a fine garden spray instead (or something similar). The results are not as good though.

These steps show how to use a proper spraygun, but the same applies to a garden spray.

Fill the spraygun container with well-mixed glaze. Place the pot on a banding wheel.

Newspaper to catch the drips.

Spray across the article as shown. Keep moving the spraygun, while slowly revolving the banding wheel at the same time.

Continue spraying until the glaze builds up as a thick dust. Stop spraying for a few seconds if any area looks wet.

Special effects

You can create all kinds of effects by using glazes in different ways. Some ideas are shown below, but you can probably think of lots more yourself.

Spatter

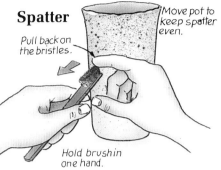

Move pot to keep spatter even.

Pull back on the bristles.

Hold brush in one hand.

Create a spatter effect by first glazing a pot all over. Then use a toothbrush, dipped in another colour of glaze, to spatter the pot as shown.

Sponging

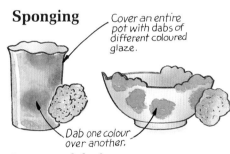

Cover an entire pot with dabs of different coloured glaze.

Dab one colour over another.

You can dab glaze on a pot with a sponge.

Masking

Leave paper in place to burn off in kiln.

Create patterns by masking areas with pieces of paper, stuck on with glue, to prevent them from being glazed. You can also do this by drawing on the pot with wax crayons (or special wax which you can buy).

Glaze firing

To finish your pots after glazing them you need to fire them, again. This is called glaze, or "glost", firing. The temperature used depends on the type of clay and glaze and is higher than for biscuit firing. You cannot fire earthenware and stoneware clay, or glazes with different firing temperatures at the same time.

Some kilns are only able to reach earthenware temperatures, so they cannot be used for stoneware.

During firing, glaze melts and spreads to make an even, glass-like coating over the ware. It is very important that the kiln is fired to the correct temperature. Glaze will bubble and run if fired too high or be very rough if fired too low. The steps on these pages show how to glaze fire.

Pots glazed all over

You must not allow any glazed surface to touch anything in the kiln, or it will stick when fired.

Points snap off (see opposite page)

Stilt

Stilts (and shelves, etc) are called "kiln furniture."

If you want to fire any pot which is glazed all over, then you can use a "stilt", like the one above, to stand it on. These stick to the pot, but snap off afterwards.

Packing the kiln

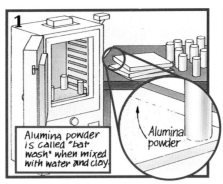

1 Alumina powder is called "bat wash" when mixed with water and clay.

Alumina powder

Remove all but the first shelf and props from the kiln. Dust the shelves with "alumina" powder* to stop any drips of glaze from sticking to them.

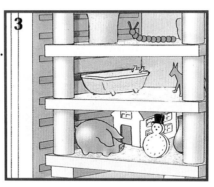

3

Add more shelves and props taking care not to spill any alumina on pots underneath. Place more pots on the shelves as you go.

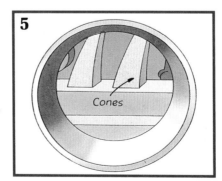

5 Cones

Work out the cones you need, if you use them, from the chart on page 33 (or the maker's chart) and position them behind the spyhole.

Warning - Pots must not touch in the kiln or they will stick together.

2 Put the tallest pots on this shelf.

Sort the pots into groups of the same height. Starting at the back, carefully place each one on the shelf so as not to touch each other or the kiln sides.

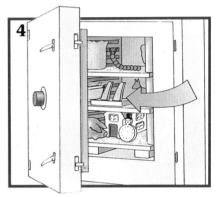

4

Continue adding pots until the kiln is full, leaving space for cones, if you use them, on a shelf level and in line with the spyhole.

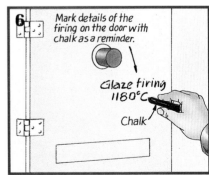

6 Mark details of the firing on the door with chalk as a reminder.

Glaze firing 1180°C

Chalk

Shut and secure the door, with a lock if possible, then follow the sequence shown on the opposite page to fire the kiln to the correct temperature.

Temperatures

The temperature you heat the kiln to depends on the clay and glazes you use.

Glaze

1020°C–1080°C

1250°C–1300°C

Glaze you buy usually has a temperature range marked on the bag or container.

Clay

1040°C–1180°C

1200°C–1280°C

The clay you buy will also often have a temperature range marked on the bag.

Suppliers also list the temperatures for clays and glazes in their catalogues. Choose a temperature between the upper and lower limits suggested for the glaze you use. The usual limits for earthenware and stoneware glaze firings are shown below.

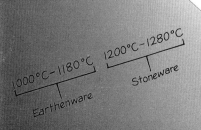

1000°C–1180°C   Earthenware

1200°C–1280°C   Stoneware

Firing sequence

It takes about 10-12 hours to reach the correct temperature for a glaze firing, depending on the kiln you use. You need to increase the temperature gradually as shown in the firing sequence below.

1 Start early in the morning. Remove the bung (see page 32). Switch on the kiln and set the temperature controller to low for about an hour.

2 Replace the bung and increase the temperature controller to its medium setting for about 5 hours.

3 Set the temperature controller to full until the final temperature is reached. Then turn the kiln off.

4 Leave the kiln for 24 hours to cool before opening the door. If you open the kiln before it has cooled below 100°C the glaze may craze.

Using stilts

These points are dangerous unless removed.

File across the points.
Mind your fingers.

If you use stilts, snap them off after firing. This leaves tiny sharp points stuck in the glaze, which you need to remove with a file or carborundum stone.

Faults checklist

Below are pictures of some common glazing faults after glaze firing. Remedies (marked with a star) are suggested to help overcome them in the future.

The picture below shows how your glaze should be.

Earthenware gloss glaze.

No cracks or bumps.

Even shiny surface (or matt if a matt glaze).

Bloating

Bubbly appearance on the clay caused by pressure from a build-up of gases when firing.

★Reduce firing temperature.

★Fire more slowly.

Crawling

Glaze forms in patches due to grease or dust on the clay, or glaze being too thickly applied.

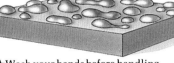

★Wash your hands before handling biscuit ware to avoid making it greasy.

★Wash dusty biscuit ware with water before glazing.

★Mix more water with your glaze.

Crazing

Fine hairline cracks all over the glaze, caused by the glaze shrinking more than the clay.

★Biscuit fire to a higher temperature.

★Try a different glaze.

★Don't open the kiln door until it has cooled.

Designing pottery

You might like to try designing your own pots after making some of the things in this book. On these pages, there are tips on how to go about doing this. The steps on the right show the stages involved in turning an idea into a finished article.

Below are some other hints which you might find useful when designing your own things. You don't have to follow all of them, but it does help to think them over when trying to decide what to do.

It is always best to think about what techniques to use before starting to make something. Things often go wrong if you start in the wrong way. You can avoid this by planning beforehand.

Ideas Don't worry about whether you think you can draw or not.

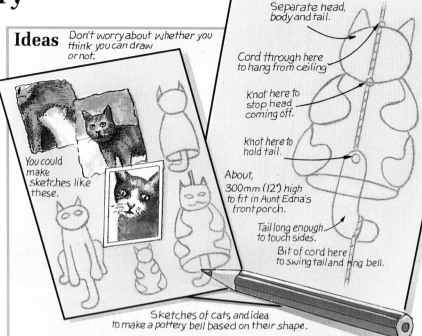

You could make sketches like these.

Separate head, body and tail.

Cord through here to hang from ceiling

Knot here to stop head coming off.

Knot here to hold tail.

About, 300mm (12") high to fit in Aunt Edna's front porch.

Tail long enough to touch sides.

Bit of cord here to swing tail and ring bell.

Sketches of cats and idea to make a pottery bell based on their shape.

First you have to have an idea, or be inspired by something. Look at pottery in shops and exhibitions for ideas. Using pictures from magazines and books also helps. Animals and natural things can often be good starting points for ideas.

Next, draw a diagram to work out how to make your idea in clay. Think about the purpose of what you want to make. If it is to use, decide whether your idea will actually do what you want it to do. If it is decorative, imagine how it might be displayed.

Shape

Imagine overall shape like this.

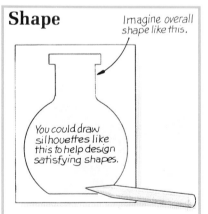

You could draw silhouettes like this to help design satisfying shapes.

When you look at a pot from a distance the first thing you see is its overall shape. When you are designing a pot, imagine this shape before thinking about any details. The intended use of a pot can be important to its shape – a tall vase for short flowers would look odd, for instance.

Proportion

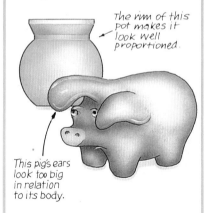

The rim of this pot makes it look well proportioned.

This pig's ears look too big in relation to its body.

Proportion means what the various parts of a pot look like in relation to each other. Imagine the parts as the pot's basic components. Then think about whether these look right together.

Edges and rims

This rim is too thin in relation to the rest of the pot.

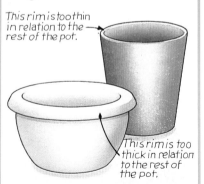

This rim is too thick in relation to the rest of the pot.

Edges are very important to the appearance of pottery, especially vases, bowls and other items with rims. Try to make edges and rims look right in relation to the rest of a pot. A thin delicate pot with a chunky rim would probably look odd, for instance.

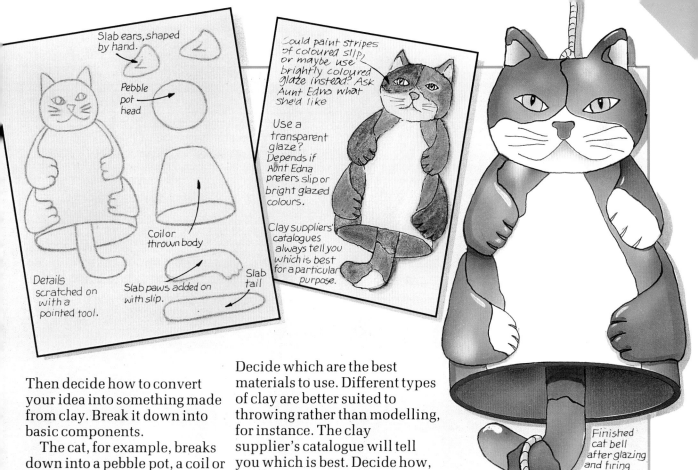

Slab ears, shaped by hand.

Pebble pot head

Details scratched on with a pointed tool.

Slab paws added on with slip.

Coil or thrown body

Slab tail

Could paint stripes of coloured slip, or maybe use brightly coloured glaze instead? Ask Aunt Edna what she'd like

Use a transparent glaze? Depends if Aunt Edna prefers slip or bright glazed colours.

Clay suppliers' catalogues always tell you which is best for a particular purpose.

Finished cat bell after glazing and firing to look like Aunt Edna's tabby cat.

Then decide how to convert your idea into something made from clay. Break it down into basic components.

The cat, for example, breaks down into a pebble pot, a coil or thrown pot and some parts made from slabs.

Decide which are the best materials to use. Different types of clay are better suited to throwing rather than modelling, for instance. The clay supplier's catalogue will tell you which is best. Decide how, and with what colours, to decorate your idea.

Decoration

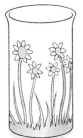

The decoration on this pot is very subtle, making it appear quiet and traditional.

This decoration is very lively, making it seem modern.

The way you decorate a pot really affects the way people react to it; whether they think it looks modern, traditional and so on.

If possible, decorate a pot so that it will fit in with the colour scheme of wherever it will be used.

Pattern

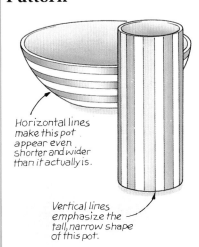

Horizontal lines make this pot appear even shorter and wider than it actually is.

Vertical lines emphasize the tall, narrow shape of this pot.

Any pattern used on a pot will affect its appearance. You can emphasize the proportions of a pot, for instance, by using horizontal or vertical lines, as shown above.

Surface and texture

This mug would be uncomfortable to use unless it had a smooth rim.

A rough texture suits the appearance of this roof

You can alter the appearance and feel of a pot by what you do to its surface – whether you make all or part of it rough, smooth or in between. Think about how a pot will be used when deciding what to do with its surface.

Selling and displaying pottery

When you have been making pottery for a while, you may be able to make things that are good enough to sell, exhibit or give away as presents. By selling your pottery, at local fairs for example, it is possible to pay for all your materials.

On these two pages there are some hints and tips to help you decide how to display, package or sell your pottery.

Craft fairs and shops

You may eventually want to try and make a living from pottery. Many people do this by selling their work at craft fairs or to shops, for example. You need to find out more about running a business if you would like to do this*. Some books to read are suggested on page 47.

Prices

Follow the three steps below to decide what to charge for your pottery. A batch of pots, like some of those explained in this book, are used as examples. Assume they were all fired together. Prices are given in numbers of coins, not in real money.

1 Fuel costs

If you are using your own kiln**, work out the cost of fuel to fire it. You only need work this out once, as each firing should take about the same time. This is how to calculate the cost for an electric kiln:

Power of kiln in kilowatts of electricity (shown on a metal plate on the kiln).

6KW

×

Price per kilowatt/hour of electricity (ask your electricity board, or look at a bill).

2 coins

×

Total number of firing hours (biscuit and glaze firing).

22 hours

Total = 264 coins

Then divide this cost roughly according to the quantity of each type of pottery fired in the kiln.

Jewellery 64 coins Piggy banks 100 coins
Desk hogs 50 coins Vases 50 coins

2 Material costs

Next work out the material costs for each type of thing you make. To do this, you'll have to make a rough guess of how much clay, glaze, and so on, that you used. Add the electricity costs to the material costs.

Material costs for 100 pairs of earrings

Clay 15 coins
Glaze 25 coins
Oxides and stains, etc
2 coins + Electricity 64 coins
Total: 15+25+2+20+64 = 126 coins

Cost per pair of earrings:
126/100 = 1·26 coins

Material costs for 20 vases

Clay 50 coins
Glaze 125 coins
+ Electricity 50 coins
Total: 50+125+50 = 225 coins
Cost per vase: 225/20 = 11·25 coins

Material costs for 30 desk hogs

Clay 45 coins
Glaze 90 coins
Electricity 50 coins

Total: 45+90+50 = 185 coins
Cost per desk tidy: 185/30 = 6·16 coins

Material costs for 40 piggy banks

Clay 65 coins
Glaze 120 coins
+ Electricity = 100 coins
Total: 65+120+100 = 285 coins
Cost per piggy: 285/40 =
7·12 coins each.

3 Profit

If you are selling pottery just to re-coup material costs you don't need to charge for your time in the price. You must if you are making pottery for a living though. To make a profit, for a charity for example, you need to charge more than the cost of materials. Start by adding what you think people would be prepared to pay, perhaps 50% more. Also add enough to cover any costs involved in selling (hiring a stall, for instance) to get your final selling price.

Earring firing and material costs:
1·10 coins per pair +50% = 1·65 coins
Vase firing and material costs:
11·25 coins each +50% = 16·87 coins
Desk hog firing and material costs:
11·25 coins each +50% = 9·24 coins.
Piggy bank firing and material costs:
7·12 coins each +50% = 10·68 coins.

What you can charge depends on how good your work is and how much people want it. You may find that after working out the price people don't buy your things. This may be because the price is too high. Try lowering the price (not below the cost of your materials) to see if this makes a difference.

*If you are selling lots of things you may have to pay tax – check with your local tax office.

**You should also take this cost into account if you are using someone else's kiln.

Display

Sales depend on an attractive display. This picture shows how you might display your pottery, either to sell, or in an exhibition.

Always try to display your pottery on different levels. You could use wooden crates or strong card boxes, covered with felt or paper, or draped with an old plain curtain.

Try not to make your display look too cluttered, or it will spoil the impact of individual pots, making them appear less attractive.

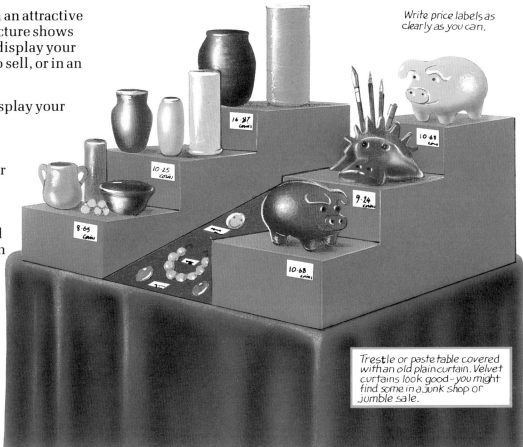

Write price labels as clearly as you can.

16·87 (coins)

10·25 (coins)

10·69 (coins)

9·24 (coins)

8·65 (coins)

10·68 (coins)

Trestle or paste table covered with an old plain curtain. Velvet curtains look good - you might find some in a junk shop or jumble sale.

Make sure curtain comes to ground level to hide table legs.

Photographing your work

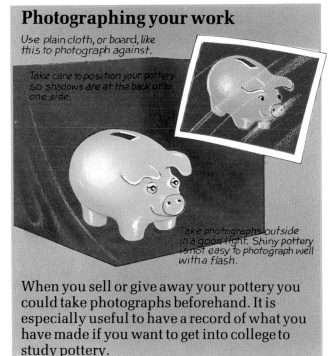

Use plain cloth, or board, like this to photograph against.

Take care to position your pottery so shadows are at the back or to one side.

Take photographs outside in a good light. Shiny pottery is not easy to photograph well with a flash.

When you sell or give away your pottery you could take photographs beforehand. It is especially useful to have a record of what you have made if you want to get into college to study pottery.

Packaging

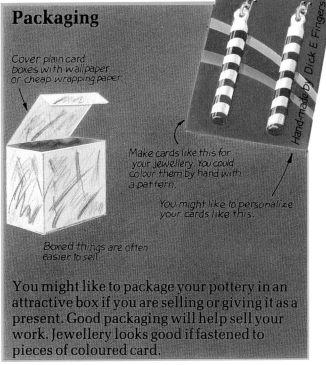

Cover plain card boxes with wallpaper or cheap wrapping paper.

Make cards like this for your jewellery. You could colour them by hand with a pattern.

You might like to personalize your cards like this.

Hand-made by Dick E. Fingers

Boxed things are often easier to sell.

You might like to package your pottery in an attractive box if you are selling or giving it as a present. Good packaging will help sell your work. Jewellery looks good if fastened to pieces of coloured card.

Colouring, re-cycling and storing materials

Here are some tips on ways of changing the colour of clay, slip and some glazes. You can also find out about re-using scrap clay and storing materials and unfinished pots.

Colouring clay and other materials

You can alter the colour of clay, slip and glaze by mixing it with a stain*. This gives the clay a colour, so it need not be glazed. This is especially useful for making jewellery. You can use transparent glaze on stained clay if you like. This gives it a deeper colour, as well as making it water resistant.

The intensity of colour depends on the amount mixed in. Use up to 1½ parts of stain to 8½ parts of clay, slip or glaze.

The finished colours of stains are brightest with white clay or slip and white or transparent glaze.
You need to work out how much stain to use in relation to the weight of material you want to mix it with.

You can do this by trial and error or use scales to weigh the ingredients. Mix a little stain at a time until the clay or slip looks the colour you want. You could make some small samples of different strengths, then fire them to see how they come out.

Follow the steps on the right to mix stains.

Scratch the amount of stain you used on the sample, so you can remember how much to use again.

1 Put the stain in a container. Add a little warm water and mix it with a stick or spoon. (Don't do this to stain large amounts of clay — see below.)

Wear a face mask to do this

Spoon
Stain

2 Glazes and slips

Pour the stain into the glaze or slip, mixing it as you go.

2 Small amounts of wet clay

Pour a little stain into a hole made in a ball of clay and gently squeeze it to mix the stain.

Stain

Make hole with your thumb.

2 Large amounts of clay

Water

Container

Let the clay dry completely, then crush it with a rolling pin. Put it in a container. Add the stain dry, mix it thoroughly, then add water. Then prepare the clay in the same way as shown in the method on the right for re-cycling clay, from step 2 onwards.

Re-cycling clay

Re-cycle all the scraps of clay left over from making things, however dry they are, by following these steps.

1 Break the clay into small pieces and put them in a bucket. Pour water over the clay and leave it overnight to soak.
2

Don't mix different types of clay in the same bucket.

Clay

Absorbent surface

Tip out any excess water and then pour the sludge onto an absorbent surface – a paving slab or block of plaster is best. (See how to make a plaster block on the opposite page.) Leave the sludge until it dries enough not to be sticky to the touch.

3 Knead, or wedge, the clay (see page 5) to remove any air bubbles and to make it a usable consistency. Do this on an absorbent surface to soak up any excess water.

Hint
To keep clay moist while working on it you can spray it with a little water from a house plant spray.

See page 35 to find out about stains and the colours you can get.

Making a plaster block

Here is a simple method for making a plaster block to roll clay on. You need an old washing up bowl (or something similar) and about 5kg (11lb) of plaster of Paris.

Plaster

1 Fill the bowl by about a third with water. Gradually sprinkle plaster on the water until it breaks the surface.

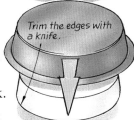

2 Mix the plaster with your hand as shown. Then tap the bowl to level it.

3 Wash your hands and leave the plaster to set overnight. Turn the bowl upside down over a table and tap it to release the plaster block.

Trim the edges with a knife.

Use the top, as the bottom will probably have ridges from the bowl.

Warning: Never get loose bits of plaster in clay – it will explode in the kiln, breaking your pottery.

Pug mills

A machine called a "pug mill" is used to mix large amounts of wet, but unwedged, clay. You may get the chance to use one if you join an evening class, for example. There are different kinds, but most work like the one shown here.

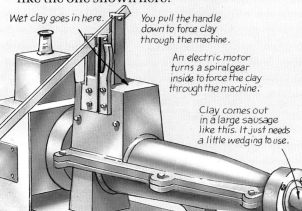

Wet clay goes in here.

You pull the handle down to force clay through the machine.

An electric motor turns a spiral gear inside to force the clay through the machine.

Clay comes out in a large sausage like this. It just needs a little wedging to use.

Storage

The tips below show how to store materials and partly finished pottery.

Clay

If you wrap clay in an air-tight plastic bag and store it in a cool place it will keep for months. It is a good idea to store large amounts in a lidded bucket.

Unfinished work

Always place unfinished work in a plastic bag or cover it with a sheet of plastic. If you want something to go leather-hard, leave it uncovered overnight, then cover it until you are ready to start work again. If you don't do this the clay may dry out too much to use.

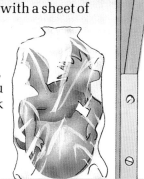

Glaze and slip

Old frozen food containers are useful for storage.

Write the glaze colour and firing temperature on the side.

It is best to store glazes, slips and other materials from which water is likely to evaporate in sealed containers. You may need to add water and re-sieve anything which dries out too much.

Red glaze
1180°-1220°C

Biscuit ware

Always cover biscuit ware, especially if it is likely to be a while before you glaze it. Any dust will spoil the glaze.

Tools, equipment and materials

Here is a complete list of all the tools, equipment and materials mentioned in this book. You can often find your nearest pottery supplier by looking in the trade pages of your telephone directory. Many companies offer a mail-order service, even for heavy materials like clay. There are some useful addresses on the opposite page.

Tools

		Metal spoon		Needle in wooden handle	
Wooden board to work on		Wooden spoon		Knitting needle	
Wooden rolling pin		Clay cutting wire		Hole Piercer	
Battens to roll clay of an even thickness		Wire-ended modelling tools		Stiff brush for slip	
Round objects to wrap clay around (e.g. bottles)		Wooden modelling tools		Soft brushes for painting	
Ruler		Sgraffito tools		Old toothbrush	
Pencil		Turning tools		Washing-up brush	
Pair of compasses		Hacksaw blade or other objects for scraping clay		Slip-trailer	
Knife		Metal kidney-shaped scrapers		Natural sponge and ordinary sponge	

Equipment

		Scales		Compressor (or compressed air in a can)	
Washing-up bowl		Dust mask		Spray booth with extractor fan	
Plastic jug		Banding wheel		Kiln (you can buy small test kilns for the price of a TV)	
Bucket		Wheel (electric or kick)		Shelves and props	
Containers for glaze and slip		Wooden bats to put pots on		Cones	
Plastic bags		Pug mill		Cone socket	
Sieve – graded to let particles of a certain size through mesh		Spraygun		Stilts	

Materials

		Coloured slip (ready-prepared)		Underglaze colours	
Clay (earthenware or stoneware)		Oxides		Alumina (for coating kiln shelves)	
Glaze (suitable for the clay you buy)		Stains		Plaster of Paris	

Pottery words and useful addresses

Banding wheel. A free-spinning circular turntable. Also called a "whirler".

Biscuit firing. The heating of clay to make it hard and porous, usually to about 980°C.

Biscuit (or bisque) ware. Unglazed, usually porous, pottery.

Coil pot. A pot made by piling sausages of clay, called coils, on top of each other.

Cone. A cone-shaped piece of ceramic material which bends at a certain temperature.

Earthenware. A type of clay, normally porous when fired to about 1140°C.

Firing. The process of heating pottery in a kiln.

Foot. A ring of clay under a pot.

Glaze. A glass-like material used to decorate pots and make them non-porous.

Glaze firing. The process of heating glazed pottery in a kiln to make the glaze melt.

Kiln. A kind of oven.

Leather-hard. Clay dried to the stage where it cuts like firm cheese.

Oxide. A chemical compound used to decorate pottery.

Pinch pot. A pot made by squeezing clay.

Pug mill. A machine for preparing clay.

Sgraffito. Scratched decoration.

Slab. A flat sheet of clay.

Slab-pot. A pot made by joining slabs of clay.

Slip. Liquid clay used for joining clay and for decoration.

Slop glaze. Ready-to-use glaze.

Stain. A colouring pigment prepared from oxides.

Stilt. A device for supporting glazed pottery in the kiln.

Stoneware. A type of clay, normally non-porous when fired.

Throwing. The process of making a pot on the wheel.

Turning. Cleaning-up the base of a pot after throwing.

Wedging. The process of kneading clay to remove air bubbles.

Wheel. A powered turntable for making pots.

Temperature conversion chart

You can use the chart below as a quick guide to convert between degrees Fahrenheit and Centigrade.

°C	°F	°C	°F
500	932	550	1022
600	1112	650	1202
700	1292	750	1382
800	1472	850	1562
900	1652	950	1742
980	1796	1000	1832
1050	1922	1100	2012
1150	2102	1200	2192
1250	2282	1300	2373
1350	2462	1400	2552
1450	2642		

You can make an exact conversion using the sums below.

Centigrade into Fahrenheit: divide by 5, multiply by 9 and then add 32 to the total.

Fahrenheit into Centigrade: subtract 32, divide the remainder by 9, then multiply by 5.

Heat-resisting wire

You can buy heat-resisting nichrome wire to fire beads which are glazed all over. Thread them on the wire, supported by a cradle of clay (as shown on page 8). This wire will not melt, unlike other types of wire.

Useful addresses

Pottery suppliers

Potterycrafts Ltd
Campbell Road
Stoke-on-Trent
ST4 4ET
England

Fulham Pottery Ltd
Burlington House
184 New Kings Road
London
SW6 4PB
England

Hammill & Gillespie Inc
PO Box 104
Livingston
New Jersey
07039
USA

The Pottery Supply House Ltd
Box 192
2070 Speers Road
Oakville
Ontario
L6J 5AD
Canada

Diamond Ceramic Supplies Ltd
50-52 Geddes Street
Mulgrave
Melbourne
Victoria 3170
Australia

Smith and Smith Ltd
73 Captain Springs Road
Box 709
Te Papa
Auckland
New Zealand

Jewellery findings

Craft'O Hans
21 Macklin Street
London
WC2B 5NH
England

Warehouse
43 Neal Street
London
WC2H 9PJ
England

Clock movement

W Hobby Ltd
Knights Hill Square
London
SE27 0HP England

Going further

You can develop your pottery techniques and learn more about the subject by attending classes or reading other books. Some books to read are suggested below.

The Potter's Manual by Kenneth Clark
Macdonald, 1983

Pottery and Ceramics by David Hamilton
Thames and Hudson, 1974

Clay and Glazes for the Potter by David Rhodes
Pitman House, 1979

Books on running a business

Introduction to Business by Janet Cook
Usborne, 1985

Setting up a Workshop by John Crowe
Crafts Council, 1982

Index

First published in 1985 by Usborne Publishing Ltd, 20 Garrick Street, London, WC2E 9BJ, England. Copyright © 1985 Usborne Publishing Ltd.

48

Printed in Belgium